MW00816802

PROUST

FOR BEGINNERS ®

PROUST
FOR BEGINNERS®

BY
STEVE BACHMANN

ILLUSTRATIONS BY
VAN HOWELL

FOREWORD BY
HAROLD AUGENBRAUM

FOR BEGINNERS®

For Beginners LLC
155 Main Street, Suite 211
Danbury, CT 06810 USA
www.forbeginnersbooks.com

Copyright ©2016 Steve Bachmann
Illustrations Copyright ©2016 Van Howell

This book is sold subject to the condition that it shall not, by way of trade or otherwise, be lent, re-sold, hired out, or otherwise circulated without the publisher's prior consent in any form of binding or cover other than that in which it is published and without a similar condition being imposed on the subsequent purchaser.

All rights reserved. No part of this publication may be reproduced, stored in a retrieval system, or transmitted in any form or by any means, electronic, mechanical, photocopying, recording, or otherwise, without prior permission of the publisher.

A For Beginners® Documentary Comic Book
Copyright © 2016

Cataloging-in-Publication information is available from the Library of Congress.

ISBN # 978-1-939994-44-8 Trade

Manufactured in the United States of America

For Beginners® and Beginners Documentary Comic Books® are published by For Beginners LLC.

First Edition

10 9 8 7 6 5 4 3 2 1

Dedication

I WOULD LIKE TO DEDICATE THIS BOOK to the oases of civilization that helped to inspire it and make it possible, *viz.*, the new and used book stores of Barcelona, Spain; Harvard Square, Cambridge; Hyde Park, Chicago; Notre Dame, South Bend; and Madison, Wisconsin. And thanks to France for planting the Albertine bookstore at Fifth and 79th in New York City.

A LSO, I WOULD LIKE TO THANK my colleagues and mentors in French: Ellen Bachmannhuff, Ruth Benner, Celia Brickman, Jacquie Erwin, Trina Hikel, and Dan Snow.

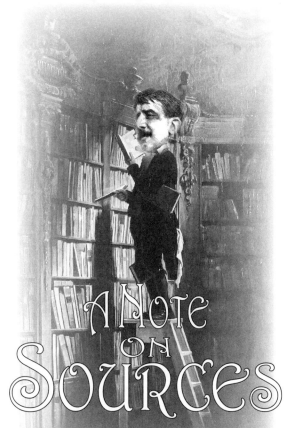

A Note on Sources

Passages quoted from *In Search of Lost Time* carry a volume and page reference (in parentheses at the end) corresponding to the relevant edition.

All passages from *Swann's Way* (Volume I) are quoted directly from the original English translation by C.K. Scott Moncrieff and Terence Kilmartin (New York: Henry Holt, 1922).

Short excerpts from the succeeding volumes (II-VI) come from the most recent revision of the full Moncrieff/Kilmartin translation, by D.J. Enright (*In Search of Lost Time.* New York: Modern Library, 1992, 1993.)

For longer passages in volumes II-VI, the author of this work has provided his own translations; in these instances, the word "see" precedes corresponding volume and page references to the Enright edition.

Similarly, short quotes from *Against Sainte-Beuve* are from Sylvia Townsend Warner's translation in *Proust: On Art and Literature* (New York: Carroll and Graf, 1984); longer passages are translated by the author of this work, with "see" referring to corresponding pages in Warner.

All other excerpts and quotations—from Proust and others—come from the sources cited in Credit Where Credit is Due or Further Reading.

Table of Contents

IN MY VIEW, THE CRITIC . . . SHOULD TRY TO RECONSTRUCT THE
PECULIAR LIFE OF THE SPIRIT WHICH BELONGS TO EVERY WRITER
WHO IS OBSESSED BY HIS OWN SPECIAL VIEW OF REALITY. . . .
[E]XISTENCE FOR HIM HAS NO JUSTIFICATION SAVE AS BEING THE
SOLE POSSIBLE MEDIUM THROUGH WHICH HE CAN MAKE CONTACT
WITH REALITY.

—MARCEL PROUST, "A MASSACRE OF CHURCHES"

Foreword
by Harold Augenbraum

During the past hundred years and more, since the 1913 publication of *Swann's Way* (in French, *Du côté du chez Swann*), Proust—his name and his works are often used synonymously—has developed a reputation for being difficult to read. "Climbing Mount Proust" is a phrase sometimes used to describe the experience.

Proust is indeed often difficult to fathom, perhaps because his style of writing is so different from that of his predecessors (he cares little for plot and less about action) or because the reach of his reference is so broad and deep. You have to work slowly. His sentences can run as long as 958 words (in translation), their subject and predicate separated by dozens of subordinate clauses. This type of stylistic "dilation," to steal a very descriptive word from poet and critic Richard Howard, adds both richness and complexity. It allows Proust to fill each passage with personal, cultural, and literary quotation and allusion, which has defined not only his writing but much of the literature of the early twentieth century, a period of great artistic foment. (James Joyce and T.S. Eliot also took the whole of their experience of civilization as a palette.) If, in an earlier age of transition, Cervantes' *Don Quixote* was flummoxed by the great adventure writers in his library of medieval tales, Proust's narrator also imbibes, embraces, and then pays homage to every one and every thing he had ever "read," which Proust himself did in his poetry, letters, pastiches, articles, and conversation, and his use of painting, architecture and music during his novel's composition.

rt is only one of Proust's universes, however. Marcel Proust lived during a period of great political and social upheaval in continental Europe. His parents were married on the day after France fell to the Prussians; the day after the wedding, France declared its Third Republic. He was born amid echoes of gunfire during the Paris Commune. If in the 1830s and 1840s his precursor, Honoré de Balzac, had chronicled the redistribution of power from France's landowners to its business élite, Proust would describe (also in fiction) the last gasp of that landed aristocracy's descent into sleaze. Three years before the publication of *Swann's Way*, Edward VII of Britain, whom Proust included as a ghostly presence in Charles Swann's social world, had been laid to rest in London in what the historian Barbara Tuchman called the last state funeral attended by the world's great monarchies—the event that marked the end of the culture of monarchy. The great nineteenth-century novelists, such as Émile Zola, would focus on commerce. Proust's interest lay not in the great fortunes and the fortunate themselves, but in the interstices, where the self-made were connected to the remnants of high society, where the transitions of many political and social eras left a rich vein of Time that Proust could explore as a fourth dimension. To Proust, mutability would become metaphor.

o call Proust a social or political novelist alone, a novelist of aesthetics, or even a novelist of Time, however, is to limit the scope of his intention. Among the great achievements of *In Search of Lost Time* (a barely adequate translation of the original French, *À la recherche du temps perdu*) are, indeed, the characters that Proust created, the embedding of the arts, real and invented, and the effects of the passage of time.

ut his true brilliance lies in the stylistically consistent and always evolving depiction of a single consciousness, set within the narrative framework of a fictionalized autobiography. Proust's narrator relentlessly layers what seems like "thinking on the page." (The section "Swann in Love," written in the third person, is an exceptions to this). He constantly reads himself—and others, if he can employ their lives in the project of understanding himself. By the time you finish the seven volumes, you want to start again from the beginning. Imagine if you could gradually recall and then put into context everything you had ever experienced, all the events of your life and then use it all to understand why you have become who you are. Reading Proust is not a blueprint for how you should live, it's a guide to reading the world. This is what the young Marcel Proust learned from the English critic John Ruskin, the hero of his early adulthood: The examined life is a function of constant observation and reiteration.

There is evidence that Proust would, had he lived beyond the age of 51, have continued to expand his novel, as he often did with individual sentences, pasting strips of paper—the famous "paperoles"—to tell transcribers and typesetters where to insert more text. Letters, marginalia, and textual alterations attest to probable further dilations of the novel's middle books. Only Proust's death interrupted his re-examinations. He died a few months after the appearance of the second volume of *Sodom and Gomorrah*, the same year Eliot's "The Wasteland" and Joyce's *Ulysses* were published. As long as consciousness continued, so did his quest to examine the examination of one of fiction's most interesting characters.

The entry into this quest with Proust and his narrator is to have a key. Proust's book begins in a series of rooms in which he unlocks themes, styles, references, and foreshadows. *Proust for Beginners* will provide that key.

Harold Augenbraum is Executive Director of the National Book Foundation, presenter of the National Book Awards, editor of the *Collected Poems* of Marcel Proust, and founder of the Proust Society of America.

Introduction

MARCEL PROUST was a French writer who lived from July 10, 1871 to November 18, 1922, and wrote a very long novel entitled *À la recherche du temps perdu* — hereafter referred to as *RECHERCHE*. His name rhymes with "boost" and "roost," not "joust" or "roust." His fame is such that he now exists not only as a noun, but also as an adjective ... a cocktail party cliché ... a style ... a legend ... and a controversy.

adjective...

A PROUSTIAN MOMENT refers to some trigger from the present that brings on a flood of memories from the distant past. Here are two examples from *RECHERCHE*:

> *On my way home ... I suddenly recalled the impression ... of which ... the cold and almost sooty smell of the trellised pavilion had reminded me. It was that of my uncle Adolphe's little sitting-room at Combray, which had indeed exhaled the same odour of humidity.* (II: 91)

> *On the first night, as I was suffering from cardiac fatigue, I bent down slowly and cautiously to take off my boots, trying to master my pain. But scarcely had I touched the topmost button than my chest swelled, filled with an unknown, a divine presence, I was shaken with sobs, tears streamed from my eyes.... I had just perceived, in my memory ... my grandmother....* (IV: 210)

Proustian Moment: Grandma's ghost found hiding in shoe

cocktail party cliché...

THE MOST FAMOUS PROUSTIAN MOMENT involves the taste of a madeleine cake dipped in tea. If you want to impress people at cocktail parties with a cliché, talk about Proust's madeleine. A madeleine is a French cupcake shaped like an oval scallop. Proust's madeleine is famous for a passage in his novel in which the author-narrator nibbles on a madeleine and is suddenly flooded with memories from his childhood.

> [My mother] sent out for one of those short, plump little cakes called "petites madeleines".... I raised to my lips a spoonful of the tea in which I had soaked a morsel of the cake. No sooner had the warm liquid, and the crumbs with it, touched my palate than a shudder ran through my whole body, and I stopped, intent upon the extraordinary changes that were taking place. An exquisite pleasure had invaded my senses, but individual, detached, with no suggestion of its origin. ... And suddenly the memory returns. The taste was that of the little crumb of madeleine which on Sunday mornings at Combray (because on those mornings I did not go out before church-time), when I went to say good day to her in her bedroom, my aunt Léonie used to give me, dipping it first in her own cup of real or of lime-flower tea. (I: 60, 63)

The encounter with the madeleine occurs only about 40 or 60 pages into the first volume of Proust's novel, depending on which edition you're looking at. When people first try to read Proust—your author included—they often give up even before reaching the madeleine incident.

style...

PROUSTIAN
SENTENCES
are known for
being long,
luxurious, and
meandering.
Here is one
sentence from
Volume I of
RECHERCE:

The name Gilberte passed close by me, evoking all the more forcibly her whom it labelled in that it did not merely refer to her, as one speaks of a man in his absence, but was directly addressed to her; it passed thus close by me, in action, so to speak, with a force that increased with the curve of its trajectory and as it drew near to its target;—carrying in its wake, I could feel, the knowledge, the impression of her to whom it was addressed that belonged not to me but to the friend who called to her, everything that, while she uttered the words, she more or less vividly reviewed, possessed in her memory, of their daily intimacy, of the visits that they paid to each other, of that unknown existence which was all the more inaccessible, all the more painful to me from being, conversely, so familiar, so tractable to this happy girl who let her message brush past me without my being able to penetrate its surface, who flung it on the air with a light-hearted cry: letting float in the atmosphere the delicious attar which that message had distilled, by touching them with precision, from certain invisible points in Mlle. Swann's life, from the evening to come, as it would be, after dinner, at her home,—forming, on its celestial passage through the midst of the children and their nursemaids, a little cloud, exquisitely coloured, like the cloud that, curling over one of Poussin's gardens, reflects minutely, like a cloud in the opera, teeming with chariots and horses, some apparition of the life of the gods; casting, finally, on that ragged grass, at the spot on which she stood (at once a scrap of withered lawn and a moment in the afternoon of the fair player, who continued to beat up and catch her shuttlecock until a governess, with a blue feather in her hat, had called her away) a mar-vellous little band of light, of the colour of heliotrope, spread over the lawn like a carpet on which I could not tire of treading to and fro with lingering feet, nostalgic and profane, while Françoise shouted: "Come on, button up your coat, look, and let's get away!" and I remarked for the first time how common her speech was, and that she had, alas, no blue feather in her hat. (I: 560–562)

legend...

Not only are Proust's sentences long. The novel itself is really, really long. One English edition tallies 1,404,975 words.

ASIDE FROM THE LENGTH of his sentences and his novel, Proust added to his legend by living weird. Most of his masterpiece was written inside a cork-lined room in Paris where Proust sequestered himself from the world. On occasion he would come out, dine at the Ritz, and leave huge tips. He hired musicians in the middle of the night to play personal concerts in his apartment. He was one of the celebrities who attended a famous Paris banquet in 1922, where he met Pablo Picasso, Igor Stravinsky, and James Joyce.

> *For the past fifteen years, I've lived in bed, I mean literally in bed, in my room, not getting up for a minute.*
>
> —**Proust**, letter, December 23, 1919

In spite of, or because of, such factors, Proust has become recognized as a modern master, reformulating the ways in which we conceptualize the world.

> *[W]e must recognize in Proust ... one of the great minds and imaginations of our day, absolutely comparable in our own time, by reason both of his power and of his influence, to the Nietzsches, the Tolstois, the Wagners and the Ibsens of a previous generation.*
>
> —**Edmund Wilson**, American critic

IF PROUST COULD BE COMPARED to the Nietzsches, Tolstois, Wagners, and Ibsens of the generation preceding Wilson's, he could also be compared to Freud, Einstein, and Picasso of his own (and Wilson's) generation. What all these towering figures had in common was an ability to discover and articulate new conceptions of human reality.

> *[W]e have to rediscover, to reapprehend, to make ourselves fully aware of that reality ... that reality which it is very easy for us to die without ever having known and which is, quite simply, our life.* (VI: 298)

controversy...

THE TITLE OF PROUST'S LONG NOVEL, *À la recherche du temps perdu*, has been variously translated as *Remembrance of Things Past*, *In Search of Lost Time*, or *On Research Into Lost Time*, depending on who is translating. (More on that later.)

"*RECHERCHE*," as we refer to it, is defined in *Cassell's French-English Dictionary* as "search, quest, pursuit; inquiry, investigation, examination, scrutiny; research, inquiries; addresses, courtship, suit...."

Proust's novel consists of some three to nine volumes, depending upon who's counting.

How to translate *RECHERCHE*'s title and how to count its volumes only begin the questions and challenges raised by this great work.

> *An American girl ... writes me that for three years she has done nothing night and day but read my books.... "I understand nothing.... Tell me in two lines what you wished to say." Since she didn't understand it in two thousand lines, or rather since I didn't know how to express it, I decided it was useless to reply.*
>
> —**Proust**, letter, December 9, 1921

> *To succeed in getting the full flavor of M. Marcel Proust, all you do indeed need to do is adopt the two main principles of physical exercise: progression and follow-through. You begin, in week one, with about twenty pages a day.... [A]t the first sign of lassitude or distraction shut the book and leave it....*
>
> —**Fernand Vandérem**, reviewer

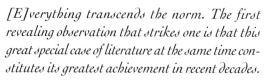

My great adventure is really Proust. Well—what remains to be written after that? ... I am in a state of amazement; as if a miracle were being done before my eyes.... One has to put down the book and gasp.

—**Virginia Woolf**, English author

[E]verything transcends the norm. The first revealing observation that strikes one is that this great special case of literature at the same time constitutes its greatest achievement in recent decades.

—**Walter Benjamin,** German literary critic

[A]ny other style compared with his appears stiff, colourless, imprescise, perfunctory and lifeless. Should I admit it? Every time I find myself bathing in this lake of delights, I do not even dare, for a good number of days afterwards, to take up my pen....

—**Andre Gide,**
French author and Nobel Prize winner

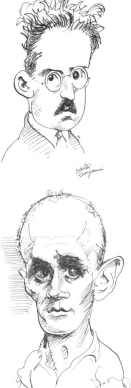

Now, I'm tranquil, I know I'm going to go from marvel to marvel.

—**Jean Genet,** French novelist and playwright

I finally finished Remembrance of Things Past and I don't know what to say—the idea that Joyce ended the novel is so absurd; it's Proust who ended the novel, simply by doing something so complete, monumental, perfect, that what the fuck can you do afterwards?

—**Andrew Holleran**, American author

Which twentieth-century artists are beyond criticism—i.e., accepted by everyone as masters to question whose status would be blasphemous? ... The only exceptions I can think of are: Chekhov and Proust—and it's stretching a point to call Chekhov a twentieth-century figure.

—**Kenneth Tynan,** English literary critic

UGH!

My dear friend, I may be dead from the neck up, but rack my brains as I may, I fail to understand why a man needs thirty pages to describe how he tosses and turns in his bed before falling asleep. **—Georges Boyer**, reviewer

They [the novels] *are the opposite of everything I like, namely, order, selection, sobriety. Technically speaking they are not books at all, but a ragbag of memories and impressions.*

—Fernand Vandérem, reviewer

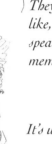

It's unreadable; the author paid the publishing costs.

—Bernard Grasset,
Proust's publisher, writing to a friend

Unsuitable for young girls.

—Ad for *RECHERCHE* by the publisher

I am reading Proust for the first time—in English of course—and am surprised to find him a mental defective.... He has absolutely no sense of time.

—Evelyn Waugh, English author

I have read the first volume of [Swann's Way], *and find it strangely uneven. There are incomparable things ... and then passages that are offensively fastidious, artificial and almost dishonest.... His loquacity is certainly more interesting and cleverly done than Moore's, but no less profuse, a maudlin false teeth gobble-gobble discharge from a colic-affected belly. I think he drank too much [tea]. And to think that I have to contemplate him at stool for 16 volumes!*

—Samuel Beckett, Irish author, Nobel Prize winner, 1929

Beckett later changed his mind about Proust and wrote one of the first serious studies of appreciation of *Recherche*.

I was re-reading the first volume of [Time Regained]. *... I disliked it before and thought it mere bourrage & badly out of control. ... Then the second volume—the last of the book—surely the first 100 pages are as great a piece of sustained writing as anything to be found anywhere. I find it more satisfactory at every reading.*

—**Samuel Beckett,** 1932

American novelist **Henry James** had it both ways when he wrote that reading Proust consisted of *"inconceivable boredom associated with the most extreme ecstasy which it is possible to imagine."*

Even Proust had his own questions about Proust.

Should I make it a novel, or a philosophical study —am I a novelist?

—**Proust**, notebook, 1908

I**N ORDER TO UNDERSTAND** P**ROUST AND** HIS WORK, it is best to start with an account of his life and times. The times were certainly changing, and so were the ways in which human beings conceived themselves.

> *The pleasure an artist gives is to make us know an additional universe.*
>
> —**Proust**, letter,
> November 1912

PART ONE
PROUST AND HISTORY

BELOW IS A MAP OF FRANCE, marked with places that will appear in this book.

= Balbec

Amiens CATHEDRAL

Laon

Le Mans

SEINE

VERSAILLES

Paris

Illiers-Combray

ALSACE

Nouvelle Carte DE A FRANCE

THREE TOPICS FROM FRENCH HISTORY help to understand Proust and his background: COMMUNES, JEWS, AND THE STATE.

Communes

INSURRECTION FOR THE COMMUNE AT CAMBRAI 958 A.D.

from a wood engraving by Alphonse Neuville 1875

In the Middle Ages, bishops and lords in France held a lot of power. As towns grew, the residents began wanting some of that power for themselves. They resisted their rulers and organized what they called communes. Here is what some of the "press agents" for the rich and powerful wrote about communes around 1100 . . .

ca. 1075, in Le Mans . . .

Yet when [Geoffrey of Mayenne] sought *to raise certain taxes against the citizens of Le Mans, and when he attempted to oppress them with certain new exactions, they gathered together to consider how they might resist his improper inclinations and how they might arrange it so that they were not unjustly oppressed by him or any other person. And when they had formed a conspiracy, which they called a commune, they all swore oaths to bind each other equally under a common obligation. Then they compelled Geoffrey himself and the other nobles of the same region, most of whom were unwilling, to be bound by the oaths of their agreement.*

—Acts of the Bishops Living in the City of Le Mans

and 1115, in Laon . . .

Now Commune is a new and a bad name *of an arrangement for all the poorest classes to pay their usual due of servitude to their lords once only in the year, and to make good any breach of the laws they have committed by the payment fixed by law, and to be entirely free from all other exactions usually imposed on serfs. ... Having therefore summoned the nobles and certain of the clergy on the last day of Lent in the holy days of the Passion of our Lord, ... [the Bishop] determined to urge the annulment of the Commune, to which he had sworn. ... The compact of the Commune being broken, such rage, such amazement seized the citizens that all the officials abandoned their duties and the stalls of the craftsmen and cobblers were closed and nothing was exposed for sale by the innkeepers and hucksters, who expected to have nothing left when the lords began plundering. ... Behold there arose a disorderly noise throughout the city, men shouting "Commune." ... There citizens now entered the Bishop's court with swords, battle-axes, bows and hatchets, and carrying clubs and spears, a very great company. As soon as this sudden attack was discovered, the nobles rallied from all sides to the Bishop, having sworn to give him aid against such an onset, if it should occur.*

—Guibert de Nogent, Benedictine monk and historian

I F ANY GROUP WAS WORSE OFF THAN SERFS and town dwellers oppressed by lords and bishops, it was Jews. French Christians hated them because they were not Christian. When they were not burning them, robbing them, extorting them, forcing them to convert, or sending them into exile, Christians tolerated Jews only because they had money that could be taxed, confiscated, or loaned out at interest (which the Church prohibited Christians from doing).

In the late 1700s, as the rationalist ideals of the Enlightenment began to spread, life for French Jews began to improve somewhat. By the 1780s, France abolished the special taxes on Jews and allowed them to do business in many enterprises from which they previously had been prohibited. The Royal Society of Science and Arts of Metz offered a prize for the best essay in answer to the question: "What are the best means to make the Jews happier and more useful in France?"

During the French Revolution, on September 27, 1791, the National Constituent Assembly voted full rights of citizenship for French Jews.

France's King
Louis XIV

(reigned 1643–1715) is said to have declared *l'etait c'est moi* ("the State is ME").

H E RULED as an absolute monarch with support from the nobles and clergy. He did not even bother to convene France's parliament, or Estates General, which had not met since 1614.

The Estates General was divided into three groups: the First Estate (clergy, about 10,000 people); the Second Estate (aristocracy, about 400,000 people); and Third Estate (everybody else, about 25 million people). Each group had one vote. Members of the Third Estate had reason to think this was unfair, since they paid most of the taxes.

T he French government lent assistance to the American Revolution from 1776 to 1783, which did not help the French treasury. By 1787, the king's government was asking the clergy and nobles to pay some taxes to help out, and they refused. In desperation, a parliament was convened. In short order (that June), the Third Estate declared that *it* really represented the French people and designated itself the National Assembly; the First and Second Estates promptly joined with them.

T he Bastille prison fell in July; feudal rights and privileges were abolished in August; and the monarchy fell in October. By year's end the new government was taking over church property, consisting of about one fifth of all the land in France.

In 1792, aristocratic Austria and Prussia threatened to invade France if it didn't protect its king and nobility. Paris responded with a Commune, and the revolutionaries raised a people's army. The king was executed with a lot of nobles and politicians, peasants, clerics, and others. In the wars that followed, an officer named Napoleon Bonaparte became general, dictator, and emperor. He took on the rest of Europe until his final defeat in 1815 at Waterloo by an alliance of Austrians, English, Prussians, and Russians, who wanted to see France returned to its older order. ⌛ ⌛ ⌛

During the next 100 years (which will bring us back to Proust!), issues associated with the French Revolution played out in various forms. For the First Estate, would the Catholic Church ever recover its privileges, or would France become more secular? For the Second Estate, would the aristocrats recover their power, or would France become more egalitarian? And for the Third Estate, how would the sometimes conflicting interests of peasants, artisans, financiers, factory owners, and factory workers—each with their own notions of democracy—be worked out?

The years 1815–1830 ("the Bourbon Restoration") saw an attempt by the aristocracy and clergy to reassert their powers. In 1830, they overreached by attempting to cut back on press freedom and an already limited electorate.

The revolution of July 1830 replaced these reactionaries with a constitutional monarch in the person of Louis-Philippe d'Orléans, who became responsible to an "expanded electorate" of 0.75% of the total population. Not surprisingly, it was a government of, by, and for the rich.

In February 1848, Louis-Philippe tried to restrict freedom of association and was toppled from power in an outburst of popular protest and street fighting. The republic that replaced him could not reconcile differences among nobles, the rich, peasants, and workers. That June, national workshops that had been set up to employ workers were shut down. The national army took care of anyone who objected, killing over 3,000, imprisoning 12,000, and deporting 4,000. In 1849, Louis Napoleon (nephew of the original) was elected to the office of president. Conservatives such as Adolphe Thiers thought they could manage "that cretin," and in 1850 attempted to cut "the vile multitude" from the voting franchise by one third (mainly workers). The factional fighting ended when Napoleon III used the army to carry out a coup d'etat in 1851. He justified it with a plebiscite in 1852, based on universal suffrage, which declared him emperor. Napoleon III ruled in authoritarian manner with the backing of his family, the army, the bureaucracy, and officially sanctioned candidates for the legislature—mainly landowners, bankers, merchants and industrialists.

It was against this background that Proust's parents were born and met each other.

FACING PAGE, TOP: MARIE ANTOINETTE BY J-L. DAVID, 1793, AND NAPOLEON BONAPARTE BY GROS, 1797. BOTTOM: STORMING OF THE BASTILLE.

THIS PAGE, TOP: NAPOLEON DEATH MASK, 1821. BOTTOM: KING LOUIS-PHILIPPE.

Proust's Parents

PROUST'S FATHER, ADRIEN, was born in 1834 to a shopkeeper in Illiers, France. The Proust family had been respectable middle-class administrators for centuries. Instead of the priesthood, Adrien determined to go to Paris to study medicine. He proved a success. By the 1860s, he was becoming an international expert on cholera. In 1869 he travelled to Russia, Persia, and Egypt to trace the course of a cholera epidemic. Upon his return to France, he was awarded the ribbon of the Legion of Honor. Around that time, as a bachelor in his mid-thirties, he encountered a young woman 15 years his junior named Jeanne Weil.

NATHÉ & ADÈLE WEIL
Maternal Grandparents

J EANNE WEIL was born in Paris in 1849. A number of Weil's family members had taken advantage of the opportunities opening up for French Jews of the era. Her father, Nathé, was a wealthy stockbroker, and his father, Baruch, had been a wealthy manufacturer. Her mother, Adèle Berncastel, came not only from money, but also from political connections and cultural sophistication.

Adèle's aunt, Amélie Crémieux, was married to Adolphe Crémieux, one of the first Jews to sit in France's Chamber of Deputies. Highly influential in national affairs, Crémieux litigated against an oath imposed on French Jews; defended the opposition press during the 1830s; participated in 1848 Revolution; served as Minister of Justice in the provisional government; abolished the

We are honored to belong to to the Israelite sect; we are Jewish French citizens.

Uncle Adolphe CRémieuX

death penalty for political crimes, imprisonment for indebtedness, and any use of the pillary; made it possible for Algerian Jews to obtain citizenship; and abolished slavery in the colonies.

"The day I'm carried to my grave," he once declared, "there's something I want said about me as I'm placed in my final resting place. I want it said, 'He was good.'" He was, and France honored Crémieux with a state funeral in 1880.

In Amélie's salon, niece Adèle met such cultural icons as Victor Hugo, Alphonse de Lamartine, Alfred de Musset, Gioachino Rossini, and George Sand. Niece Adèle absorbed everything and conveyed it to her daughter Jeanne. Aunt Amélie eventually converted to Catholicism, taking her children with her.

Rossini, Sand, and Hugo at Amélie's salon

Politics and the Birth of Proust

OTH ADRIEN PROUST AND JEANNE WEIL were ambitious, progressive, and secular. Adrien had social standing and a future; Jeanne had culture and money. The couple signed a marriage contract on August 27, 1870, and sealed the bond with a civil ceremony in Paris on September 3. Jeanne agreed to raise her children Catholic, but declined to renounce her Judaism.

Religious controversy in France would not interfere with the marriage of Jeanne Weil and Adrien Proust. The former believed only in reason; the latter refused to take an oath in court under a crucifix.

Politics, however, both internationally and within France, proved more problematic. The following timeline puts Proust's family history **(marked in bold)** — including his own conception and birth — in historical context:

May 8, 1870: Napoleon III wins plebiscite, affirming his "liberal reforms."

July 2, 1870: Spain announces it will accept Prince Leopold, a relative of Wilhem I of Prussia, as its king.

July 6, 1870: France objects to the prospect of being surrounded by German kingdoms. The French Foreign Minister threatens war, declaring: "We shall know how to fulfill our duty without hesitation and without weakness."

July 7: French police informer writes: "This war will generate wide enthusiasm and rally the whole of France behind the Napoleonic dynasty; this war will deal the final blow to the republican cause in France."

July 11: French ambassador asks Prussian King Wilhelm I to withhold consent from Leopold's accession. Wilhelm agrees.

July 12: Napoleon commiserates to his Prime Minister: "The country will be disappointed, but what can we do?"

July 13: French ambassador asks Wilhelm to promise he will never consent to a relative being a candidate for the Spanish throne. Wilhelm refuses. Opportunistic Prussian Chancellor Bismarck releases a provocative version of the events in the "Ems Telegram."

July 14: Ems Telegram widely published in France on Bastille Day. French public explodes.

July 19: France declares war on Prussia.

August 1870: Following his research on cholera, Dr. Adrien Proust does medical inspections at entry points into France.

August 27: Adrien Proust and Jeanne Weil sign marriage contract.

September 1, 1870: Prussians crush French Army at Battle of Sedan.

September 1: Adrien Proust takes residence in the heart of Paris.

September 2: Napoleon III surrenders himself and his army to the Prussians, then dissolves his Second Empire.

September 3: Adrien Proust and Jeanne Weill marry in civil ceremony.

September 4: France declares the Third Republic.

September 19: Prussians begin Siege of Paris.

October 10, 1870 (est.): Adrien and Jeanne conceive Marcel Proust
(below)

November 30, 1870: Parisians fail attempt to break Prussian siege.

December 1870: Early cold, severe winter. Poor eat dogs and cats to survive, rich get camel hump and zoo elephants.

December 27: Prussians bombard Paris outskirts.

January 5, 1871: Prussians bomb Paris proper.

January 19: Another attempt to break the siege fails. Bread rationing begins in Paris.

January 26-28: France agrees to an armistice, Siege of Paris ends.

February 8, 11, 1871: French elect National Assembly which in turn elects Adolphe Thiers (the guy who had done so well managing "that cretin" Napoleon III) as head.

March 1-3, 1871: Prussians march into Paris, march out after armistice ratification.

March 18: Thiers attempts to disarm Paris National Guard and take its artillery. Parisians resist, Paris Commune begins.

April 2, 1871: Thiers begins bombing Paris.

April 2 (approx.): Sniper shoots at Adrien Proust; he moves with his family to the Parisian suburb of Auteuil.

May 10, 1871: Prussians and French sign Treaty of Frankfurt, allowing release of French prisoners and doubling of Thiers' army from 55,000 to 120,000.

May 21–28: Thiers' troops break into Paris; 20,000 Parisians are killed and/or executed.

June 10, 1871: "The smell of bodies disgusts me less than the miasmas of egoism breathed from every mouth." —Gustave Flaubert to George Sand.

July 10, 1871: Marcel Proust is born.

⧗   ⧗   ⧗

CONTEMPORARY MEDICINE SUGGESTS THAT A FETUS gestating under stressful conditions is vulnerable to further health issues after birth. Certainly the fetus of Marcel Proust was subjected to stress, and the life of Marcel Proust was marked by compromised health (asthma, insomnia, fevers) and behavior considered unusual. Concerning Marcel and his younger brother Robert, Proust scholar William Carter has written: "Robert, like many second children, experienced none of the difficulties and traumas of the first. The family always believed that the younger brother had the advantage of being conceived and born in a stable time."

LEFT & ABOVE: LITHOGRAPHS BY HONORÉ DAUMIIER C. 1871

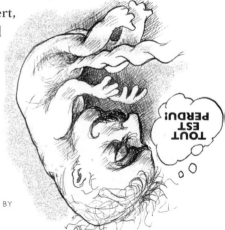

TOUT EST PERDU!

Destabilization and the Modern

IF MARCEL PROUST CAME INTO THE WORLD under conditions of stress, the world he entered was itself destabilizing. Some called it modernization. Various artists reacted to the tenor of the times with their own destabilized and destabilizing works. Here are some of the things happening in Western culture and technology during Proust's formative years:

1871: Eugène Pottier and Pierre De Geyter compose the socialist anthem, "L'Internationale."

1872: James McNeill Whistler paints *The Artist's Mother*.

1873: Typewriter invented (Remington & Sons); Arthur Rimbaud's *A Season in Hell* published.

1874: First Impressionist exhibition.

1875: George Bizet's opera *Carmen* debuts.

1876: Alexander Graham Bell invents the telephone.

1877: Thomas Edison invents the phonograph.

1879: Henrik Ibsen's *A Doll's House* premieres; Thomas Edison patents his electric lightbulb.

1880: Fyodor Dostoevsky's *Brothers Karamazov* completed *(left)*.

1881: Le Chat Noir, the first modern cabaret, opens in Paris.

1882: World's first hydroelectric power plant opens in Wisconsin; Hiram Maxim invents the first portable, automatic machine gun. Death of Charles Darwin *(below left)*.

1883: Friedrich Nietzsche *(below right)* publishes *Thus Spoke Zarathustra*.

1884: Odilon Redon, Georges Seurat, and Paul Signac found the neo-impressionist Society of Independent Artists.

1885: Karl Benz invents the single-cylinder motor car engine.

1886: Last Impressionist exhibition; Jean Moréas publishes the *Symbolist Manifesto*.

1887: Hannibal Goodwin invents celluloid film.

Proust was perfectly unfit for a world unfitting itself.

Young Proust

I T WOULD BE BOTH MELODRAMATIC AND INACCURATE to say that Proust had a miserable childhood. He loved and was loved by his mother, grandmother, and brother. He enjoyed family vacations in the suburbs of Paris, his father's hometown (Illiers), and the coast of Brittany. He did well in school, made friends, and founded literary journals with them.

1884 YOUNG PROUST WRITES AN ESSAY:

> *Literary studies allow us to disdain death, they lift us above earthly things by speaking to us about spiritual matters.*

1886 YOUNG PROUST ANSWERS A QUESTIONNAIRE:

Your favorite occupation?

Reading, daydreaming, poetry, history, theater.

Your idea of unhappiness?

To be away from Mummy.

Where would you like to live?

In the realm of the ideal, or rather of my ideal.

For what fault have you most toleration?

For the private lives of geniuses.

Teenage Proust and the Late 1880s

In 1888, George Eastman invented the Kodak box camera; Vincent Van Gogh and Paul Gauguin painted in Arles; Friedrich Nietzsche published *Twilight of the Idols* and *The Antichrist*; and August Strindberg wrote the naturalistic stage drama *Miss Julie*.

In 1889, Nietzsche went mad; the Crown Prince of Austria committed suicide with his mistress; philosopher Henri Bergson published *Time and Free Will*; Santiago Ramón y Cajal isolated the neuron; and the Eiffel Tower was erected in Paris for the World's Fair.

In 1890, Paul Verlaine published explicit erotic poems entitled *Women*. Van Gogh committed suicide.

TEENAGER MARCEL PROUST, MEANWHILE, was wrestling with his libido. He masturbated so much that his father gave him 10 francs to go to a brothel. It didn't work out.

On May 17, 1888, Proust wrote his grandfather:

I am appealing to your kindness for the sum of 13 francs.... Mama prefers I ask you.... Papa gave me 10 francs to go to the brothel. But (1) in my addled state I broke a chamber pot, 3 francs, (2) in this same state I wasn't able to fuck.

Two snapshots of Private Proust of the 76th Infantry Regiment

In the meantime, he propositioned some of his male friends at school.

That fall, Proust wrote a friend:

> *I am glad to say that I have some highly intelligent friends, distinguished by great moral delicacy, who have amused themselves with a boy....*

And on October 2, Proust wrote his philosophy teacher, Alphonse Darlu:

> *I can no longer take complete pleasure in what used to be my highest joy, the works of literature. ... [E]ven while I am savouring the infinite delights of former days, my other self examines me ... and ends by killing nearly all my pleasure.*

From 1889 to 1890, despite questionable health, Marcel served in the French army.

CLOSE-UP OF ARMY SNAPSHOT ABOVE LEFT

Early 1890s

WHEN MARCEL LEFT THE ARMY, he was 20 years old. It was time to find a career. Younger brother Robert was seeking a medical degree, like their father. Marcel enrolled in the Free School of Political Science, Diplomatic Section. He enrolled in law school.

Marcel also studied philosophy, tutored by his "hero," Alphonse Darlu. A teacher at the Lycée Condorcet, Darlu was something of a Platonist. Platonists believed that Ideals are real and that objects are real only to the degree that they reflect the Ideal. The chair one sits on is not as real is the Ideal Chair it reflects.

Marcel the young philosopher wrote essays with sentences like these:

It is the Spirit that structures matter.

The spirit must be more than a phenomenological object. The idea of phenomenon is itself something that is beyond the phenomena. The whole does not lie in the phenomenon.

This page: Prof. Darlu prepares a lesson

Facing page: Fernand Gregh

30

1892: Proust answers another questionnaire:

My main character trait. The need to be loved; more precisely, a need to be petted and spoilt more than a need to be admired.

The quality I want to see in a man. Feminine charm.

My favourite quality in a woman. The virtues of a man, and openness in friendship.

My dream of happiness. I'm afraid it would be sufficiently elevated; I daren't express it, and I'm afraid of destroying it by expressing it.

What my greatest unhappiness would be. Not to have known my mother or my grandmother.

My heroes in real life. Monsieur Darlu, Monsieur Boutroux.

The military action I most admire. My voluntary service!

In 1892, Marcel founded a literary journal with some friends, including Fernand Gregh. They called it *Le Banquet*, after Plato's *Symposium*. Concerning Proust, Gregh observed:

He sometimes exaggerated this grace in mincing but always witty ways, just as at times he used to exaggerate his amiability in excessive but always intelligent flattery; and we even made up among ourselves the verb "to proustify" to express an attitude that was just a bit too conscious of its niceness with a touch of what the vulgar mob would have called "la-de-da nonsense" that was delicious and went on nonstop.

Marcel Proust
EARLY 1890s

Below left: Circa 1892, Robert de Flers, Lucien Daudet, and Marcel Proust
Art credit for Proust's thought goes to Proust himself (from a doodle on a manuscript page).;

Below right:: Count Montesquiou

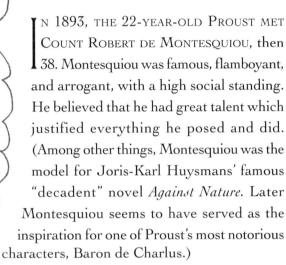

I N 1893, THE 22-YEAR-OLD PROUST MET COUNT ROBERT DE MONTESQUIOU, then 38. Montesquiou was famous, flamboyant, and arrogant, with a high social standing. He believed that he had great talent which justified everything he posed and did. (Among other things, Montesquiou was the model for Joris-Karl Huysmans' famous "decadent" novel *Against Nature.* Later Montesquiou seems to have served as the inspiration for one of Proust's most notorious characters, Baron de Charlus.)

I discovered long ago that you stood far above the type of exquisite decadent with those features (never as perfect as yours, but common enough in these times) you are depicted. In this period devoid of thought and will, indeed without genius, you excel through your double power of thought and action.

—Proust, letter to Montesquiou, April 24, 1893

33

I N 1894, PROUST MET THE 19-YEAR-OLD MUSICIAN REYNALDO HAHN, and the two became lovers. Hahn describes walking in a garden with Proust:

> *I found him at the same place, staring at the roses. His head tilting forward, his face very serious, he blinked, his eyebrows slightly furrowed as though from a passionate act of attention, and with his left hand he was obstinately pushing the end of his little black mustache between his lips and nibbling on it. ... How many times I've observed Marcel in these mysterious moments in which he was communicating totally with nature, with art, with life, in these "deep minutes" in which his entire being was concentrated....*

Marcel Proust was becoming a Parisian man about town, a fashionable dandy frequenting salons, writing articles, taking vacations, and meeting society people. He was not cut out for a career in law and detested the prospect.

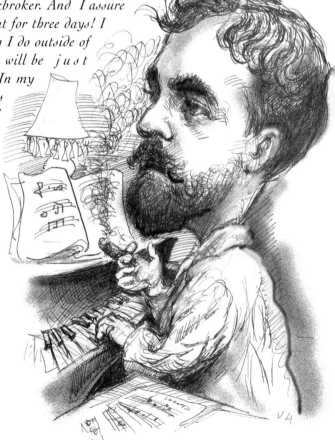

As for a law office, I should vastly   prefer going to work for a stockbroker. And I assure you, I wouldn't stick it out for three days! I still believe that anything I do outside of literature and philosophy will be j u s t so much time wasted. ... In my most desperate moments I have never conceived of anything more horrible than a law office.

—Proust,
letter to father,
September 28, 1893

In 1895, Marcel secured employment as a librarian. He spent much of his time on leave, however, and left that job in 1900.

Mid-1890s: First Book

In 1896, William Ramsay discovered helium, Ernest Rutherford discovered electrical waves, A.H. Becquerel discovered radioactivity, German artists discovered *art nouveau* and called it *Jugendstil*, and Strindberg was hospitalized for psychosis.

Claude Monet was in the middle of his series paintings in which he represented one subject many times, exploring how different it looked during different parts of the day or the year. (*Haystacks*, 1890–91; *Poplars*, 1892; *Cathedral at Rouen*, 1892–94; *Normandy Cliffs*, 1896; *Seine*, 1896–97; *Giverny Japanese Bridge*, 1899)

In 1896, Alfred Jarry's play *Ubu Roi* opened in Paris with the word *merde*. Audiences riot, and the play closes.

Véritable portrait de Monsieur Ubu.

ALSO IN 1896, MARCEL PROUST PUBLISHED HIS FIRST BOOK, a collection of short stories entitled *Pleasures and Days*, with drawings by MadeleineLemaire.

ABOVE: "True Portrait of Monsieur Ubu" by Alfred Jarry

RIGHT: Title page by Madeleine Lemaire (that's her house, where Proust met Hahn)

LEFT: Reynaldo Hahn

LES PLAISIRS

ET

LES JOURS

THE NOTED FRENCH WRITER ANATOLE FRANCE contributed an introduction:

What a fortunate book is his! It will go all around the town adorned and perfumed by the flowers strewn on it by Madeleine Lemaire, with that divine hand which scatters the roses with their dew.

And Proust's stories included declarations such as these:

[I]t is better to dream your life than to live it. (116)

Detest bad music if you will, but don't despise it. ... The irritating refrain, for instance, that any refined and well-trained ear will immediately refuse to listen to, has been the repository for the riches of thousands of souls, and keeps the secret of thousands of lives, for which it was the living inspiration, the ever-ready consolation, always lying half-open on the piano's music stand—a source of dreamy grace for those lives, and an ideal. (127)

The habit to which you are sacrificing me again this evening will be even stronger tomorrow thanks to the blood from the wound that you are inflicting on me to nourish it. . . . [A]lready I barely exist any more. I am your soul, I am yourself. (132)

Left: ANATOLE FRANCE

36

PROUST & FRIENDS
CONVERSE BEFORE
DINNER IS SERVED

from an illustration
in "Les Plaisirs et les jours"
by Madeleine Lemaire

PLEASURES AND DAYS prompted a scathing review by Jean Lorrain (aka Paul Duval):

> *There is no beating the fashionable set. ... A book perpetrated by one of their kind ... has come into my hands....* Les Plaisirs et les jours, *by M. Marcel Proust: suave melancholic reveries, elegiac languishings, elegant and refined little trifles, shallow emotions, inane flirtations in precious and pretentious tones, together with Mme Lemaire's flowers, scattered symbolically.*

In response, Proust challenged Lorrain to a duel. It took place on February 6, 1897, with injuries to neither party.

Take that!

DUVAL
Returns
FIRE!

PROUST MAY HAVE REALIZED that Lorrain made one good point in that *Pleasures and Days* had been printed in a deluxe edition of 1500 copies at 15 francs a pop. Proust's publisher refused to try a 3.50 franc edition until the deluxe edition had sold out. By 1918, 1,171 copies remained unsold.

> Les Plaisirs et les jours ... *these are pages written at school, when I was fifteen years old, as is only too obvious.*
>
> —Proust, letter, February 14, 1918

Madeleine Lemaire delivered her illustrations for ***Pleasures and Days*** two years late. Proust returned the favor by immortalizing her quirksiness in the absurd character of salon hostess Madame Verdurin in *Recherche*.

Mid~1890s : Anti-Semitism and the Dreyfus Affair

Dreyfus the Traitor by V. Lenepveu (pseudonym, true identity unknown), from his Musée des Horreurs poster series 1899-1900. Lorraine Beitler Collection of the Dreyfus Affair, University of Pennsylvania Libraries,.

In 1896, AS THE U.S. SUPREME COURT sanctioned state-sponsored segregation in its *Plessy v. Ferguson* ruling, European racists were oppressing Africans in Africa. At home, they reverted to the old evil of anti-Semitism. In Vienna, the anti-Semitic demagoguery of Mayor Karl Lueger inspired a young Adolf Hitler. Lueger disgusted a young Jewish writer named Theodor Herzl,

Herzl

TOP LEFT (INSERT):
Lueger's "Hunting Season"
Vienna newspaper, September, 30 1893.

FACING PAGE: Esterhazy

who published a book in 1896 titled *The Jewish State*. In it he argued that Jews would be safe only if they had their own country.

Herzl had been led to this conclusion not only by Austrian politics. He had also been in Paris to cover the Dreyfus Affair, where he might have hoped for the more "sophisticated" French to demonstrate more civilized behavior. Many of them did not.

THE DREYFUS AFFAIR, which lasted 12 years, began in 1894 when a French military officer named Ferdinand Esterhazy began selling military secrets to the Germans. French Intelligence got wind of the matter. Idiots and anti-Semites at French military HQ decided that the real culprit was Captain Alfred Dreyfus, who happened to be Jewish. In a closed session, Dreyfus was court-martialed on bogus evidence. The French anti-Semitic press had a field day.

In 1895, Dreyfus was publicly court-martialed and sent to the penal colony on Devil's Island. In the meantime, a new person was appointed to head French Intelligence, Lt. Colonel Georges Picquart.

In 1896, Picquart came to the conclusion that Dreyfus was innocent and was promptly transferred to Tunisia. Dreyfus' supporters agitated in the press, and the conspirators began manufacturing more bad evidence.

Yesterday I did not answer the question you put to me about the Jews. For this very simple reason: though I am a Catholic like my father and mother, my mother is Jewish. I am sure you understand that this is reason enough for me to refrain from such discussions.

— Proust, letter to Montesquiou,
May 19, 1896

The year 1897 saw public agitation over the Dreyfus case continue to grow. The French Army responded by convening a convenient court-martial for Major Esterhazy.

41

I N 1898, THE AFFAIR ERUPTED into a scandal. On January 10, the closed kangaroo court-martial began, and the next day it unanimously cleared Esterhazy. Picquart was then arrested for passing military secrets. On January 13, the famous writer Émile Zola published his famous *"J'accuse"* letter. In it he charged the government with illegal conduct and cover-up in its handling of the Dreyfus Affair:

I ACCUSE THE WAR OFFICE of using the press, particularly L'Eclair and L'Echo de Paris, to conduct an abominable campaign to mislead the general public and cover up their own wrongdoing.

Finally, I accuse the first court martial of violating the law by convicting the accused on the basis of a document that was kept secret, and I accuse the second court martial of covering up this illegality, on orders, thus committing the judicial crime of knowingly acquitting a guilty man. ...

I have but one passion: to enlighten those who have been kept in the dark, in the name of humanity which has suffered so much and is entitled to happiness. My fiery protest is simply the cry of my very soul. Let them dare, then, to bring me before a court of law and let the enquiry take place in broad daylight! I am waiting.

O N J ANUARY 15, A PUBLIC PETITION calling for a retrial appeared in the newspaper *Le Temps*. The petition was signed by such luminaries as the director of the Pasteur Institute, Emile Duclaux, painter Claude Monet, and sociologist Emile Durkheim. Proust also signed the petition, and proved instrumental in securing the signature of Anatole France.

> *I signed the first of the petitions on behalf of Dreyfus, and ... I was an ardent Dreyfusard, sending my first book to Picquart in his Cherche-Midi prison.*
>
> —Proust, letter, December 1919

The Dreyfus Affair continued through 1906 in a succession of lawsuits, forged documents, trials, retrials, reconvictions, resignations, demonstrations, riots, public assaults, assassination attempts, duels, suicides, flights to England, reinvestigations, appeals, and reversals.

*f*INALLY, IN JULY 1906, BOTH DREYFUS AND PICQUART were exonerated and reinstated in the military. The remains of Émile Zola, who had died in 1902, were interred in the Panthéon. On July 20, Dreyfus was enrolled in the Legion of Honor in the same courtyard where he had been disgraced. Supporters cried, "Long Live Dreyfus!" He responded, "No, gentlemen, no, I beg of you. Long Live France!"

Col. Picquart in 1913

The Dreyfus scandal split France, especially between secular republicans and conservative Catholics. Everyone had to have an opinion and everyone did. Even family members were divided. Robert Proust agreed with his brother Marcel that Dreyfus was innocent, but their father Adrien was loath to accept anything critical of the French establishment that had treated him so well.

Proust remained loyal to his Jewish heritage, yet felt conflicted when republicans pushed secularist measures too far for his taste.

I should have had to say that I wasn't a Jew and I didn't want to do that.

— Proust, letter, May 29, 1905

Lt. Col. (retired) Alfred Dreyfus
born 9 Oct. 1859, Mulhouse, France
died 12 July 1935, Paris
with his favorite granddaughter, Madeline Levy

Jean Santeuil

MARCEL PROUST PARTICIPATED in the Dreyfus Affair but was not consumed by it. In 1895, he began work on a novel he never finished, titled *Jean Santeuil*. In true Proustian fashion, he managed to generate around 300,000 words. This unfinished work was eventually published in 1952.

The interest in *Jean Santeuil* today is primarily a function of what Proust achieved later. In it, Proust still seems to be wrestling with his subject matter, his style, and his vision. Aside from providing suggestive anecdotes concerning his own biography, *Santeuil* offers intimations of Proustian themes to come, particularly those relating to the madeleine experience and how sensations from the mundane present can precipitate divine eruptions from the past, if not from another reality.

It needs but a dismal autumn day when the sun sets unseen, a road drying after rain, or the coming of the earliest winter chills, to make us drunk on the remembered beauty of the past and the primal substance of our lives. (274)

So often seeking beauty in a mountain or a sky we find it again in the sound of rubber-tired wheels or the smell of a scrap of fabric ... wrenching ourselves free from the slavery of the now, letting ourselves be flooded with the feeling of life everlasting. (410)

[A] perfume smelled in the past time, a remembered light shining into our room, will suddenly bring back [the concentrated essence of ourselves] so vividly, that it fills us with a species of intoxication, so that we become completely indifferent to what is usually called "real life" ... a sense of passionate ecstasy being the only sign by which we can recognize the truth of the ideas that flow in upon us. (464)

Late
JOHN RUSKIN 1890s:

I N 1897, J.J. THOMSON DISCOVERED THE ELECTRON, Marie and Pierre Curie discovered radium, and Ernest Rutherford discovered alpha and beta rays. Stéphane Mallarmé dispensed with punctuation and typeface consistency in his poem "A Dice Throw At Any Time Will Never Abolish Chance." Max Weber suffered a nervous breakdown. The following year, Gauguin attempted suicide. ⧖ ⧖ ⧖

IT WAS AROUND THIS TIME that Proust discovered the English art critic, social critic, and proto-environmentalist John Ruskin (1819–1900).

> *If ever you send me fragments of letters or passages from Ruskin, what interests me most at the moment is what he wrote about the French cathedrals other than Amiens—apart from* The Seven Lamps of Architecture, The Bible of Amiens, Val d'Arno, *the* Lectures on Architecture and Painting, *and* Praeterita, *because I know these books by heart.*
> —Proust, letter, February 7-8, 1900

Ruskin wrote things like this:

> *To see clearly is poetry, prophecy, and religion—all in one. Life without Industry is sin, and Industry without Art, brutality.*
> —Ruskin, *Modern Painters*

> *I believe the right question to ask, respecting all ornament is simply this: "Was it done with enjoyment—was the carver happy while he was about it?"*
> —Ruskin, *The Seven Lamps of Architecture*

> *It is not that men are ill fed, just that they have no pleasure in the work by which they make their bread, and therefore look to wealth as the only means of pleasure.*
> —Ruskin, *The Stones of Venice*

> *From what we have seen to be its nature, we must, I think, be led to one most important conclusion: that wherever the human mind is healthy and vigorous in all its proportions, great in imagination and emotion no less than in intellect, and not overborne by an undue or hardened pre-eminence of the mere reasoning faculties, there the grotesque will exist in full energy.*
> —Ruskin, *The Stones of Venice*

THE LAST YEARS OF RUSKIN'S LIFE were marked by dementia, deterioration, and disintegration. He did manage to write one final work, an autobiography called *Praeterita*. Its title, content, and style all seem to have influenced Proust directly.

> *Who could possibly have told your friend that I was translating* Praeterita *and the parts of Ruskin's correspondence and journal that the publishers added to it?*
>
> —Proust, letter, early 1907

The title, *Praeterita*, is Latin for "past things," not unlike *temps perdu* or "lost time."

In terms of content, *Praeterita* is not exactly a memoir but a collection of memories.

> *I have written ... speaking of what it gives me joy to remember, at any length I like ... and passing in total silence things which I have no pleasure in reviewing....*
>
> —Ruskin, *Praeterita*, Preface

> *I have allowed this tale ... to be thus chance told, because I think my history will, in the end, be competent if I write as its connected subjects occur to me, and not with formal chronology of plan.*
>
> —Ruskin, *Praeterita*

In terms of style, Ruskin's sentences wander about like his memories.

> *Ruskin is the master of the long sentence in English, the inclusiveness of the periods matching the range of his preoccupations. One is scarcely surprised to learn that Proust knew* Praeterita *by heart.*
>
> —Clive Wilmer

Proust also discovered a technique of composition, dependent upon memory, which Ruskin had employed before but never so effectively. The elusive unity of Praeterita *stems from a series of linked images....*

—John Rosenberg

Ruskin died on January 20, 1900, and Proust was deeply saddened.

[W]hen I learned of Ruskin's death, I wished to acquaint you before anyone else with my sadness, a wholesome sadness, let me say, replete with consolation, for I am shown how paltry a thing death is when I see how vigorously this dead man still lives, how I admire him, listen to him, and make a greater effort to understand him than I do a good many of the living.

—Proust, letter, January 21, 1900

PROUST WAS SO TAKEN BY RUSKIN AND HIS WORK that he translated *The Bible of Amiens* (1904) and *Sesame and Lilies* (1906), along with annotations and introductions.

The Bible of Amiens

FROM PROUST'S PREFACE: *I had said to myself, in my enthusiasm for Ruskin: ...*
He will purify me, for his inspiration is like the lily of the valley. He will intoxicate
me and will give me life, for he is the vine and the life. ...

[A]esthetic pleasure is given to us in addition if we love Beauty for itself as something
*real existing outside of us, and infinitely more important than the joy it gives us.... *
Ruskin was one of those men ... warned of the presence near them of an eternal reality,
intuitively perceived by inspiration, ... to which they dedicate their ephemeral life in
order to give it some value.... It is the power of genius to make us love a beauty more
real than ourselves.... (27, 33, 59)

Sesame and Lilies

FROM PROUST'S PREFACE: *So long as reading is for us the inciter whose magic*
keys open to our innermost selves the doors of abodes into which we would not have
known how to penetrate, its role in our life is salutary. But, on the other hand,
reading becomes dangerous when instead of waking us to the personal life of the spirit,
it tends to substitute itself for it.... (118)

[Ruskin] passes from one idea to another without any apparent order. But in reality
the fantasy which leads him follows its profound affinities which in spite of himself
enforce upon him a superior logic. So that in the end he happens to have obeyed a kind
of secret plan which, unveiled at the end, imposes retrospectively on the whole a sort of
order and makes it appears magnificently arrange up to this final apotheosis. (146)

RUSKIN SAMPLE: *It is simply and sternly impossible for the English*
public, at this moment, to understand any thoughtful writing — so in-
capable of thought it has become in its insanity of avarice. ... No book is
worth anything which is not worth much; nor is it serviceable until it has been
read, and re-read, and loved, and loved again; and marked, so that you can refer
to the passages you want in it, as a soldier can seize the weapon he needs in an
armoury, or a housewife bring the spice she needs from her store. (274–275)

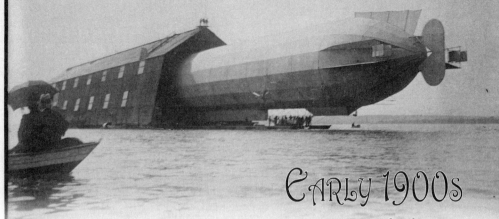

€ARLY 1900s

W HILE PROUST WAS WORKING WITH RUSKIN, science and culture pro-
ceeded apace. In 1900, Max Planck announced his quantum theory,
Ferdinand von Zeppelin made his first airship flight, Sigmund Freud
published his *Interpretation of Dreams,* and Theodor Dreiser published his
naturalistic novel *Sister Carrie.* In 1901, philosopher Edmund Husserl
launched the study of phenomenology to investigate *Erlebnisstrom,* or "the
stream of experience." The year 1901 saw the appearance of Strindberg's
dark drama *The Dance of Death,* followed by Anton Chekhov's naturalistic
Three Sisters in 1902. The Wright brothers made their first successful airplane flight in late 1903. In 1904, Max Weber published *The Protestant Ethic
and the Spirit of Capitalism* and Marie Curie published her essay *Recherches
sur les substances radioactives* ("Research on Radioactive Substances"). Two
of Ludwig Wittgenstein's brothers committed suicide in 1902 and 1904,
and Viennese artist Gustav Klimt painted a wedding portrait of Ludwig's
sister Margaret in 1905.   ⌧   ⌧   ⌧

€VEN IN DEATH, Ruskin continued to influence Proust's life and work.
Marie Nordlinger, a cousin of musician Reynaldo Hahn, had been
helping him translate Ruskin's writings. For Christmas 1898, he wrote
her an unmistakably Proustian holiday greeting:

> *And while little by little Christmas has lost its truth for us as an anniver-
> sary, it has at the same time, through the gentle emanation of accumulated
> memories, taken on a more and more living reality, in which candlelight.*

Many thanks to Dan Grossman of airships.net for scanning and sharing this gem from his photo collection

... [T]he smell of its tangerines imbibing the warmth of heated rooms, the gaiety of its cold and its fires, the scent of tea and mimosa, return to us overlaid with the delectable honey of our personality, which we have unconsciously been depositing over the years during which—engrossed in selfish pursuits—we paid no attention to it, and now suddenly it sets our hearts to beating....

In 1900, perhaps inspired by Ruskin, Proust took two trips to Venice. In 1902 he travelled to Holland, where he was smitten with Vermeer's seventeenth-century painting *View of Delft:*

Ever since I saw the "View of Delft" at the Museum of the Hague, I knew I had seen the most beautiful picture in the world....

—Proust, letter, May 1921

IN FEBRUARY 1903, Proust served as best man at his brother's wedding. As a cousin later recalled, he wore three overcoats, a number of mufflers, and a tuxedo stuffed with cotton wool. In the church, he announced loudly and repeatedly that he had to dress that way because he had been sick for months. As soon as he was able, he retreated to his bed, claiming a fever and sore throat.

HIS FATHER died that November.

⌛ ⌛ ⌛

Above: Father Adrian with brother Robert
Right: Proust bundled up
redrawn from a sketch made by his friend Jean Cocteau

Thoreau

In January 1904, Proust discovered the writings of Henry David Thoreau (1817–1862).

> *[I read] the admirable pages from* Walden. *... It's as though one were reading them inside oneself so much do they arise from the depths of our intimate experience.*
>
> —Proust, letter, January 15, 1904

      ⌧   ⌧   ⌧

The passages that resonated with Proust may well have included these:

Heaven is under our feet as well as over our heads.

[B]e a Columbus to whole new continents and worlds within you, opening new channels, not of trade, but of thought. Every man is the lord of a realm beside which the earthly empire of the Czar is but a petty state, a hummock left by the ice.

It is remarkable how easily and insensibly we fall into a particular route, and make a beaten track for ourselves. ... How worn and dusty, then, must be the highways of the world, how deep the ruts of tradition and conformity.

Sainte-Beuve

I N DECEMBER 1904, France marked the centennial of one of its most celebrated
literary critics, Charles-Augustin Sainte-Beuve (1804–1869). Proust was
not an admirer.

> *[O]ne may say that Sainte-Beuve did not appreciate any of the great writers*
> *of his time. ... This blindness of Sainte-Beuve, in regard to his time, contrasts*
> *singularly with his pretentions to insight, to foreknowledge.*
>
> —Proust, Preface to *Sesame and Lilies*

Nor was Proust alone in his opinion.

> *Sainte-Beuve ... As a critic, without any standard, steadiness, and backbone,*
> *with the cosmopolitan libertine's tongue for a medley of things, but without*
> *the courage even to confess his libertinage. As a historian, without philosophy,*
> *without the power of the philosophical eye....*
>
> —Friedrich Nietzsche, *Twilight of the Idols*

⌛ ⌛ ⌛

IF FRANCE'S CELEBRATION of Sainte-Beuve got Proust's dander up, the death
of his mother the following year did much to bring him down.

> *She takes away my life with her, as Papa had taken away hers.*
> —Proust, letter, September 27, 1905

> *Only one thing has been spared me. I haven't had the torment of dying before*
> *her and experiencing the horror that that would have been for her.*
> —Proust, letter, September 28, 1905

In December 1906, Proust moved to a new apartment at 102 Boulevard
Haussmann in Paris.

*I've sub-rented an apartment in our house in the boulevard Haussmann,
where Mama and I often came to dine, and where together we saw our old
uncle die in the room that I shall occupy. Of course I shall be spared nothing—frightful dust, trees under my window, the noise of the boulevard. ... If
I can't stand it I shall leave.*

—Proust, letter, October 9, 1906

Late 1900s

Anyone got the time? I can't take much more of this!

Folks'll spend the rest of the 20th Century wondering what to make of the weird ideas we're having right now.

Virginia Woolf once wrote that "on or about December 1910, human character changed." She hedged her bets by adding that "the change was not sudden and definite like that. But a change there was, nevertheless; and, since one must be arbitrary, let us date it about the year 1910."

Woolf might just as well have picked 1905, when Einstein announced his Theory of Relativity, Matisse and the Fauves first exhibited in Paris, and the German Expressionists organized themselves into *Die Brücke* in Dresden.

OR 1906, when Paul Cézanne died, Félix Fénénon published three-line novels in Paris, and Australia released the world's first full-length feature film, *The Story of the Kelly Gang*. Or when Mark Twain tried writing his *Autobiography* and began wrestling with the problems of articulating consciousness:

> *And that is because life does not consist mainly — or even largely — of facts and happenings. It consists mainly of the storm of thoughts that is forever flowing through one's head.* (January 10, 1906)

> *Dear me, the power of association to snatch mouldy dead memories out of their graves and make them walk!* (March 7, 1906)

> *[T]he thoughts which swarm through our heads are almost constantly, almost continuously, accompanied by a like swarm of reminders of incidents and episodes of our past.* (January 6, 1907)

OR 1907, when Picasso painted *Les Demoiselles d'Avignon*, the Lumière brothers invented color photography, and Pope Pius X condemned modernism.

OR 1908, WHEN HELIUM WAS LIQUIFIED, ammonia synthesized, and plastic invented, when Geroges Braque's *Houses at L'Estaque* (and related works) were called bizarreries cubiques ("cubic oddities"), and when Arnold Schoenberg premiered his atonal Second String Quartet.

OR 1909, WHEN WASSILY KANDINSKY produced his first abstract painting, Italian artists published their Futurist Manifesto, and James Joyce revealed the draft of a novel (*Portrait of the Artist as a Young Man*) that opened like this:

Once upon a time and a very good time it was there was a moocow coming down along the road and this moocow that was coming down along the road met a nicens little boy named baby tuckoo...

IN THE MIDDLE OF ALL THIS, PROUST had begun groping toward the path that would finally lead him to *RECHERCHE*. His progress can be tracked in letters:

July 27, 1907: *As for Ruskin, I've ceased to translate him.*

February 2, 1908: *I'm anxious to settle down to a fairly long piece of work.*

May 5–6, 1908: *In any case I'm not sure I won't abandon my Parisian novel.... For I have in hand:*
> *A study on the nobility*
> *A Parisian novel*
> *An essay on Sainte-Beuve and Flaubert*
> *An essay on women*
> *An essay on pederasty (not easy to publish)*
> *A study on stained-glass windows*
> *A study on tombstones*
> *A study on the novel*

Mid-August, 1909: *I am finishing a book which in spite of its provisional title* Against Sainte-Beuve, Memory of a Morning, *is a genuine novel and an extremely indecent one in places. ... The book does indeed end with a long conversation about Sainte-Beuve and about aesthetics ... and once people have finished the book they will see (I hope) that the whole novel is simply the implementation of the artistic principles expressed in this final part, a sort of preface if you like placed at the end....*

Arnold Schoenberg

THOMAS HARDY

As the decade drew to a close, Proust discovered a book by English novelist Thomas Hardy (1840–1928).

I have just been reading something very beautiful which unfortunately slightly resembles what I am doing (only it is a thousand times better): The Well-Beloved *by Thomas Hardy. It doesn't even lack that slight touch of the grotesque which is an essential part of all great works.*

— Proust, letter, December 1909

Hardy's *The Well-Beloved* concerns a successful sculptor named Jocelyn Pierston. As Plato postulated the reality of the ideal chair, which manifests itself in "ordinary" reality through many versions of the ideal chair, so Hardy postulated the reality of an ideal beloved, who manifests herself in "ordinary" reality through many versions. In the novel, Hardy writes:

To [Jocelyn's] Well-Beloved *he had always been faithful; but she had had many embodiments. Each individuality known as Lucy, Jane, Flora, Evangeline, or what-not, had been merely a transient condition of her.*

In *The Well-Beloved*, Jocelyn's Well-Beloved resides mainly in the bodies of three generations of women—Arice, Ann Arice, and Arice. Jocelyn manages to love and lose all of them: Arice, the eventual grandmother, when he is in his 20s; Ann Arice, the daughter of Arice and mother of Arice, when he is in his 40s; and the "final" Arice, when he is in his 60s.

Hardy later noted that he found echoes of his Platonism in Proust:

The theory on which this fantastic tale of a subjective idea was constructed is explained in the Preface ... the theory of the transmigration of the ideal beloved one, who only exists in the lover, from material woman to material woman—as exemplified also by Proust many years later.

THE CORK-LINED ROOM

IT WAS AROUND this time as well that Proust had his bedroom at 102 Boulevard Haussmann lined with cork to block out construction noise from a nearby apartment.

I had arranged to have some alterations which are essential for my peace and quiet done to my room in Paris, but as I kept writing to my architect "I may come back tomorrow," they were unable to get down to work. ... [M]y life is so bizarre and lamentable that whenever I talk about it I give the impression of apologizing.

—Proust, letter,
December 31, 1909

Oh dear... He's CORKED! ...PERDU!

Oui, VERY CORKED indeed... He's had too much of TIME!

Against Sainte-Beuve

MEANWHILE, PROUST PUSHED AHEAD on his literary fragments, which continued to expand in his notebooks. Although they were probably completed in 1909, they were not discovered until after Proust's death. They were later assembled for publication and appeared as a 300-page book in 1954 under the title *Against Sainte-Beuve*.

⧗　　⧗　　⧗

Against Sainte-Beuve might be viewed as a first sketch, or a warm up, for *RECHERCHE*. In the first pages, Proust begins discussing his experiences with "resurrections":

That which the intellect provides us under the name of the Past is not the Past. In reality, as happens to the souls of the departed in some popular legends, each hour of our lives, once it has died, becomes embodied in a material object and hides there. ... There is a country house where I have spent several summers of my life. Sometimes I thought on those summers, but those reflections were not them. There was a good chance that those summers would always remain dead to me. Their resurrection hung, like all resurrections, on mere chance. The other night, returning frozen by the snow, and not able to warm myself, while I had begun to read in my room under the lamp, my old cook proposed to me to make a cup of tea, which I never take. As chance would have it, she brought me some slices of toast. I dipped the toast in the cup of tea, and at the moment when I put the toast in my mouth and when I had the sensation of its softness penetrated with a taste of tea against my palate, I felt a disorder, of smells of geraniums, of oranges, a sensation of extraordinary light, of happiness; I sat immobile, fearing that a lone movement would stop that which had passed in me and which I still did not comprehend, and I concentrated on the piece of dipped bread which seemed to produce all the marvels, when suddenly the shaking walls of my memory yielded, and there appeared the summers I spent in that country house which I said had flooded my consciousness, with their mornings, bringing with them a procession, an incessant load of happy hours. Then I remembered: all the days, when I had dressed, I descended into the room of my grandfather who just awakened and took his tea. He dipped a zwieback and gave it to me to eat.... Compared to this past — the intimate essence of ourselves — the truths of the intellect seem a very trivial reality. (see 19–20, 24)

Working Toward Swann

In his cork-lined bedroom beginning in 1909, Proust began shaping his initial narrative fragments into the novel that would become *Recherche*—and then continued writing. He reported his progress and conundrums in letters to friends.

May–June 1911: *I am always expecting my book to end and it is not yet finished.*

March 21, 1912: *My book will be between eight and nine hundred pages long.*

November 1912: *I believe that the 1st volume ... to which a subtitle will be given; for example, general title* Les Intermittences du coeur [The Alternatings of the Heart]; *1st volume, subtitle:* Le Temps perdu [Lost Time]; *second volume, subtitle:* L'Adoration perpetuelle [The Perpetual Adoration], *or perhaps* A l'ombre des jeunes filles en fleur [In the Shadow of Young Girls in Flower]; *3rd volume, subtitle:* Le Temps retrouvé [Time Recovered].

☒　☒　☒

Finally, on November 14, 1913, the first volume of Proust's long work was published under the title *Du côté de chez Swann.*

Proust may have had an easier time writing the book than finding a publisher for it. Originally he had wanted the first volume to be published by *Nouvelle Revue Française (NRF)*, a leading literary journal run by, among others, André Gide. *NFR* refused, however, in part because they thought Proust was a jerk. Other publishers also rejected the manuscript, so Proust decided to print the book through Bernard Grasset using his own money. Grasset suggested that the novel be sold for 10 francs; Proust insisted on a price of 3.50 (along with a lower royalty), perhaps because of his experience with *Pleasures and Days*. Most of all, he said, he did not want his "thoughts to be reserved for people who spend ten francs on a book and are generally stupider than those who buy them for three...."

Once *Swann* appeared in print, *NFR* realized it had made a mistake. Gide wrote Proust an apology:

THE REJECTION OF THIS BOOK *will remain the gravest mistake ever made by the NRF—and (for I bear the same of being largely responsible for it) one of the most bitterly remorseful regrets of my life. ... [I recalled you] as the man who wrote for the [conservative newspaper] Figaro. I thought of you—shall I confess it?—as belonging to the Verdurin clan: a snob, a dilettante socialite—the worst possible thing for our review.*

A CONTRITE ANDRÉ GIDE

WAR
Interruptus

THINGS WERE FINALLY STARTING TO LOOK UP. But before Proust could see his second volume published, a Serbian nationalist assassinated the heir to the throne of Austria-Hungary, Archduke Franz Ferdinand, on June 28, 1914. In the tinderbox of European affairs, the incident ignited what came to be called the Great War, or World War I. The four years of conflagration cost the lives of up to 10 million soldiers and almost as many civilians. The rulers of Germany, Austria-Hungry, Russia, and the Ottoman Empire were overthrown, and the Austro–Hungarian and Ottoman Empires were dissolved.

⧗ ⧗ ⧗

DURING THE WAR YEARS, Proust worked on revising and expanding his book, and found a way to make *NFR* his publisher. He also gathered a number of articles and sketches he had written over the years and had his new publisher issue them under the title *Pastiches et Mélanges*.

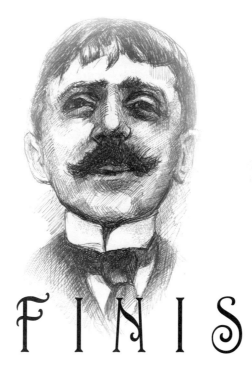

FINIS

World War I ended on November 11, 1918, and the rest of Proust's volumes began appearing in print almost immediately:

- November 30, 1918: *À l'ombre des jeunes filles en fleurs*
- 1920: *Le Côté de Guermantes I*
- 1921: *Le Côté de Guermantes II — Sodome et Gomorrhe I*
- 1922: *Sodome et Gomorrhe II*

Marcel Proust

from his last photograph Alive

EARNING CRITICAL ACCLAIM and international celebrity for the initial volumes, Proust famously attended a dinner at the Majestic Hotel in Paris in May 1922, joined by such other leading lights of European modernism as Pablo Picasso, Igor Stravinsky, Serge Diaghilev, and James Joyce.

Said Joyce: *Proust shows life as analytical and immobile. The reader finishes his sentences before he does.*

The year 1922 was also notable for the publication of *Swann* in English, translated by the Scottish writer C.K. Scott-Moncrieff.

Said F. Scott Fitzgerald: *Scott-Moncrieff's Proust is a masterpiece in itself.*

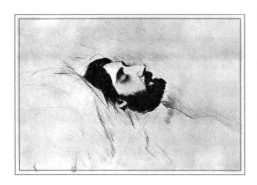

PROUST was correcting proofs for succeeding volumes when his chronic asthma developed into pneumonia. He died on November 18, 1922, attended by his maid, Céleste Albaret, and his doctor and brother, Robert.

SUBSEQUENT YEARS saw publication of the remaining sections of *RECHERCHE:*

- 1923: *Sodome et Gomorrhe III — La Prisonnière*
- 1924: *Albertine disparue*
- 1927: *Le Temps Retrouvé*

ILLUSTRATIONS:

Above: Igor Stravinsky

Below: Paul Helleu's deathbed study of Proust

Part Two
Recherche

Now it's time to look at Proust's masterwork itself—at least after some preliminary points concerning What, Who, Where, When, and How...

What?

ONE OF THE FIRST ISSUES that comes up in discussing RECHERCHE is how to divide the work. The mélange of *Le Côté de Guermantes One and Two, Sodome et Gomorrhe One, Two, and Three*, can be confusing, to say the least.

The French seem to have settled on dividing *RECHERCHE* into seven volumes. In the United States, it tends to be served up in six books. (English versions have combined *The Captive/Prisoner* and *The Fugitive* into a single volume.) At present, there are two full versions of *RECHERCHE* available in the United States— an "early" version initially translated by Scott-Moncrieff and his successors, and a later, amended Scott-Moncrieff version, published by Modern Library.

We will discuss *RECHERCHE* according to the American volume breakdown and introduce each with various title options, according to the following system:

A la recherché du temps perdu
(On the Research of Lost Time, On Research Into Lost Time)

In Search of Lost Time (later Moncrieff title)

In Search of Lost Time (Penguin title)

Remembrance of Things Past (early Moncrieff title)

Auf der Suche nach der verlorenen Zeit (German title, from Suhrkamp)

Who?

The major "who" question for *Recherche* concerns the narrator. *Recherche* is told mainly in the first person. Commentators often refer to that person as "the Narrator," although he might also be referred to as Marcel, because there is at least one paragraph in *Recherche* in which the Narrator is twice addressed by that name (V: 202–203). Readers will note, of course, that Marcel happens to be the name of *Recherche*'s author, Marcel Proust. Proust would probably insist that Proust the author be differentiated from the narrator of his book, since *Recherche* is a philosophical novel, not an autobiography.

But because I had the misfortune to begin a book with the word "I", people jumped to the conclusion that, instead of seeking to uncover laws in general, I was undertaking "self-analysis," in its most personal and detestable sense.

—Proust, letter, October 1921

However, even Marcel Proust the author sometimes refers to himself as the personal, self-narrating voice of *Recherche* in letters to various friends.

You will see [Albertine] when she is just "a young girl in bloom," in whose shadow I spend such happy hours at Balbec. Then when I become suspicious of her over nothing at all and then, for no good reason, either, I trust her again … I arrive at a point of wishing for her death … I learn of Albertine's death….

—Proust, letter, late 1915

Accordingly, we will refer to the first-person narrator of *Recherche* as Marcel, as well as the Narrator.

The more minor "who" question for *Recherche* also involves "real" identities. Just as *Recherche*'s fictional Marcel Narrator begins with Real-Life Marcel Proust, so one can trace many major characters from *Recherche* to actual people from real life. Such endeavors have amused Proust fanatics for years.

Where?

RECHERCHE takes place mainly in three locations in France:

COMBRAY

BASED ON PROUST'S FATHER'S HOMETOWN OF ILLIERS, SOUTHWEST OF PARIS

BALBEC

BASED ON CABOURG,
A SEASIDE RESORT IN NORMANDY

and

PARIS

BASED ON PARIS

When?

One could do worse than to set *RECHERCHE* within the exact parameters of Proust's life, 1871–1922, or in a fifty-year period such as 1875–1925. One researcher, Willy Hachez, calculated that Marcel Narrator was actually born in 1879 and derived other dates in *RECHERCHE* from that. In our discussion of each section, following Hachez, we will try to give a sense of the "actual historical time" in which the story is taking place.

How?

It is hard to write a synopsis of any work of fiction. For example, one might summarize two major works of Western literature—Homer's *Odyssey* and James Joyce's *Ulysses*—in just four words, "How I got home," or, better, sixteen words, "A guy trying to go home encounters problems and adventures before finally reaching home and wife." And yet, much as these brief synopses pertain to both works, each of them differs in matters of language, style, details, themes, approach, and focus. In how much detail must one delve into these aspects in order to convey a full sense of each work? In the end, of course, to get a full sense of the work in question, one should read the whole darn book.

Nevertheless, teachers and critics continue to try to cull and compress Homer and Joyce. And we will try to do something similar with Proust. So we begin with a sixteen-word synopsis: "A guy who wants to write figures out something worth writing about and writes about it."

In five words, the summary might be as simple as: "How I became a writer."

The structure of *RECHERCHE* is circular. It begins with a young man wanting to be an author. In its final pages, the author finally realizes that he has a book in him worth writing, and he sits down to write it. Thus, from the last page of the last volume, one returns to the first page of the first volume. The first sentence of the first volume reads as follows:

> *For a long time I used to go to bed early.* (I: 1)

And the last sentence of the last volume concludes with these words:

> *... they touch the distant epochs through which they have lived, between which so many days have come to range themselves—in Time.* (VI: 532)

Part of Proust's tactic is to link the last sentence of his book with the first by using the word "time" in each, reflecting a tactic he noted in 1907:

> *Thus the word parricide, having opened the article, closed it.*
> —Proust, letter, February 1, 1907

AND SO LET US BEGIN our attempt to recapitulate Marcel's research of, and search for, Lost Time.

Swann's Way

Du côté de chez Swann
Swann's Way (later Moncrieff)
The Way by Swann's (Penguin)
Swann's Way (early Moncrieff)
Unterwegs zu Swann

Years: 1890, 1880, 1895

O NE SCARY THING about *Swann's Way* is that almost all of the many major characters of *RECHERCHE* make an appearance in this first volume. The problem for the reader is that it is not clear who will become important or how they will develop. One could argue that the reader should begin *RECHERCHE* with the final volume, because it is there that one is alerted to who and what will finally be deemed important; everything one reads in the earlier volumes will really end up somewhere, in something that climaxes in something quite meaningful. As Proust explained in letters to friends:

August–September 1913: Not only is it impossible to anticipate the whole work from this single volume, which derives its meaning from the others.... it will be like those pieces which, when played separately at a concert, we fail to recognize as leit-motive *until later when we are able to place them in the work as a whole....*

February 24, 1913. There is a Monsieur who narrates and who says "I"; there are a great many characters; in the first volume they are "prepared" in such a way that what they do in the second is exactly the opposite of what one would expect from the first. ... [I]t is so complex that it will not be clear until much later where all the "themes" have begun to be combined.

With due respect to the many, many (literally hundreds of) characters in *Recherche*, the following stand out as playing major roles:

Swann Family:

Gilberte Swann is a contemporary of Marcel Narrator (born around 1880). She is the daughter of Charles Swann, a rich Jew, and of Odette, a social climber with a dubious reputation caused by a dubious history. (Odette begins her married life as Mme. de Crécy, and then becomes Mme. Swann, then Mme. de Focheville.) Around 1902, Gilberte marries Marquis Robert de Saint-Loup-en-Bray (whom we meet in Volume II), and they produce a daughter, Mlle. Saint-Loup (whom we meet in the final volume).

Guermantes Family:

The Guermanteses derive from the nobility around Combray; they also reside in Paris. There are the Duke and the Duchess Guermantes (Basin and Oriane), and the Prince and the Princess Guermantes (Gilbert and Marie-Hedwig). Robert Saint-Loup is a nephew to Oriane as well as to Baron Charlus, who is a brother to Basin.

The Verdurin Circle:

Mme. Verdurin rules over a salon and becomes Princess Guermantes when Marie-Hedwig dies. Various characters attend her salon. Artists that pass by or through this "little clan" in one fashion or another include Bergotte the novelist, Elstir the painter, and Vinteuil the composer.

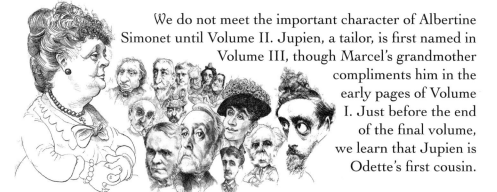

We do not meet the important character of Albertine Simonet until Volume II. Jupien, a tailor, is first named in Volume III, though Marcel's grandmother compliments him in the early pages of Volume I. Just before the end of the final volume, we learn that Jupien is Odette's first cousin.

Marcel Narrator also has a mother, a father, a grandmother, and a grandfather; the family has a cook named, Françoise. The novel begins with the young narrator (about 10 years old, around 1890) in Combray, trying to get to sleep and finagle a goodnight kiss from his mother as his elders try to entertain Charles Swann, a neighbor. Marcel's mother reads to him from George Sand's *François le Champi*.

Marcel mulls over memory:

> *And so it was that, for a long time afterwards, when I lay awake at night and revived old memories of Combray, I saw no more of it than this sort of luminous panel. ... The past is hidden somewhere outside the realm, beyond the reach of intellect, in some material object (in the sensation which that material object will give us) which we do not suspect....* (I: 56, 57–58)

It is at this juncture that Marcel has his madeleine moment, with its flood of sensations:

> *[I]n that moment all the flowers in our garden and M. Swann's park, and the water-lilies on the Vivonne and the good folk of the village and their little dwellings and the parish church and the whole of Combray and of its surroundings, taking their proper shapes and growing solid, sprang into being, town and gardens alike, from my cup of tea.* (I: 62)

MARCEL TURNS TO RECOLLECTIONS OF COMBRAY, the name of which provides the title of the first section of *Swann*. There are two paths that Marcel and his family and friends usually take as they walk about Combray: one goes toward Méséglise-la-Vineuse, past Swann's estate; thus it known as "the Méséglise Way," or "Swann's Way." The other goes toward the chateau of the local nobility, the Guermantes family; hence it known as "the Guermantes Way." For your cocktail conversation or French Lit seminar, here is an opportunity to observe that Swann's Way represents life with the high bourgeoisie, and that Guermantes Way represents life with the French aristocracy. Marcel Narrator explored both.

Swann in Love
Gilberte, Odette, Charlie

Vinteuil, who has recently died, taught piano to Marcel's family. At one point, Marcel finds himself watching Vinteuil's daughter with a friend in what might be a lesbian frolic; they discuss spitting on a photograph of her father.

At another juncture, while travelling in the countryside, Marcel catches sight of two church steeples in Martinville. He experiences a "special pleasure, which bore no resemblance to any other" and, "overpowered by a sort of intoxication, … could no longer think of anything but them." He tries to write about the experience and thinks he has succeeded "as though I myself were a hen and had just laid an egg." (I: 247–250)

In Swann's second section, "Swann in Love," we move back in time to around 1879 and Swann's affair with Odette. His emotions ride a roller coaster, in part because of himself, in part because of the nature of love, and in part because Odette has a colorful past. A "little phrase" from a sonata by Vinteuil becomes an "anthem" for their love.

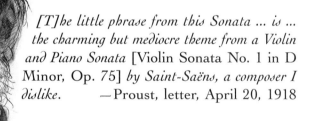

[T]he little phrase from this Sonata … is … the charming but mediocre theme from a Violin and Piano Sonata [Violin Sonata No. 1 in D Minor, Op. 75] *by Saint-Saëns, a composer I dislike.* —Proust, letter, April 20, 1918

IN THE THIRD, relatively short section, titled "Place Names—The Name," Marcel has come to Paris. Swann and Odette have married, and their daughter Gilberte has been born (around the same time as Marcel, 1880). Marcel experiences feelings for Gilberte.

Within A Budding Grove

À l'ombre des jeunes filles en fleurs

Within a Budding Grove (later Moncrieff)

In the Shadow of Young Girls in Flower (Penguin)

Within a Budding Grove (early Moncrieff)

Im Schatten junger Maechenbluete

Years: 1896–1897, Narrator 16–17 years old, to 1898.

THIS VOLUME HAS TWO PARTS, "Madame Swann at Home," and "Place Names — The Place." The first part traces Marcel's variegated and ultimately futile course of love with young Gilberte. The Swann household otherwise attracts him because there he meets the novelist Bergotte, who can discuss literature with him, and because there he can be infatuated with Mme. Swann. None of this prevents Marcel from allowing his creepy Jewish school friend Albert Bloch from taking him to a brothel where he might enjoy the charms of the Jewess Rachel. (Bloch: "Think of that, my boy, a Jewess! Wouldn't that be thrilling? Rrrrr!") When Marcel meets Rachel, he finds that her boudoir contains a couch resembling one belonging to his Aunt Léonie, and the memories it rouses prevent him from performing.

While Marcel waits for Françoise to use a public water closet, the air around the entrance triggers another version of his madeleine moment. The "cool, fusty smell" fills him with a "pleasure that was solid and consistent, on which I could lean for support, delicious, soothing, rich with a truth that was lasting, unexplained and sure." (II: 88) Marcel correlates it to a humid odor from his Uncle Adolphe's sitting room in Combray.

IN THE SECOND PART OF *GROVE*, two years have passed since Marcel's passion for Gilberte. He takes a vacation in Balbec with his grandmother, who encounters a childhood friend named Mme. Villeparisis. She happens to be a Guermantes and introduces Marcel to her nephew, Baron de Charlus, and great nephew, Robert Saint-Loup.

Marcel finds Baron Charlus strange, and things will grow even stranger. Saint-Loup's gentlemanly character is contrasted to that of Bloch, who is seen trying to advance his reputation through anti-Semitic imprecations and claiming to have enjoyed the charms of Mme. Swann. And while Marcel finds Saint-Loup accommodating, he is led to conclude that "friendship is … an abdication of self. Even conversation, which is friendship's mode of expression, is a superficial digression which gives us nothing worth acquiring." (II: 664)

ABOVE: One of various Paris public toilets photographed by C. Marville (1813–79).

RIGHT: Gustave Moreau, one of several contemporary artists on whom Proust is believed to have modeled his Elstir character.

Marcel meets also meets a painter named Elstir, who leads him to further thoughts on artistic creation:

> [I]f God the Father had created things by naming them, it was by taking away their names or giving them other names that Elstir created them anew. The names which designate things correspond invariably to an intellectual notion, alien to our true impression.... (II: 566)

SKETCH FOR SELF-PORTRAIT AS CHIMERA
DISPUTED ATTRIBUTION TO MOREAU

A ND THROUGH ELSTIR, Marcel meets a young lady whom he had encountered earlier with a group of young girls. Her name is Albertine Simonet. For the time being, she refuses to kiss him.

ABOVE: Claude Monet, said to be another inspiration for "the famous artist Elstir."

MARCEL ALSO EXPERIENCES two more madeleine moments. The sight of three trees in Hudimesnil precipitates a singular "profound happiness," and Marcel concludes that "in attaching myself to the reality of that pleasure alone could I at length begin to lead a true life." (II: 404, 405) Near Balbec, Marcel is "touched to the heart" in an encounter with a hawthorn bush. (II: 684–685)

The Guermantes Way

Le Côté de Guermantes (The Guermantes Way)

The Guermantes Way (later Moncrieff)

The Guermantes Way (Penguin)

The Guermantes Way (early Moncrieff)

Guermantes

Years: 1898–1899, Narrator about 18 years old

IN *THE GUERMANTES WAY*, we return to Paris. Marcel, it happens, is now living in "a flat forming part of the Hôtel Guermantes." (III: 3) In the courtyard of the hotel, Marcel notes that Jupien is keeping a tailor shop.

In this volume, Marcel has shifted his infatuation to the Duchess Guermantes and her high society. Aside from the death of Marcel's grandmother, most of *Guermantes Way* is about Marcel's experience in high society. Among other things, he finds that Saint-Loup now has Rachel as a mistress (and is supporting Dreyfus). When Charlus insults him, Marcel responds by stomping on Charlus' hat.

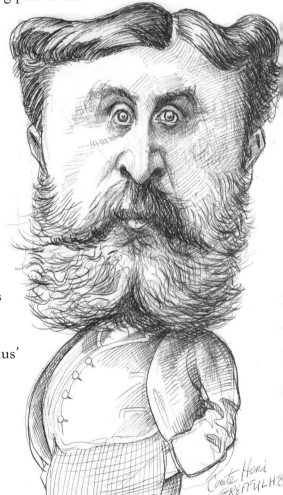

Proust's Duke and Duchess Guermantes closely resembled the Count and Countess Greffulhe

In the end, Marcel finds high society inadequate:

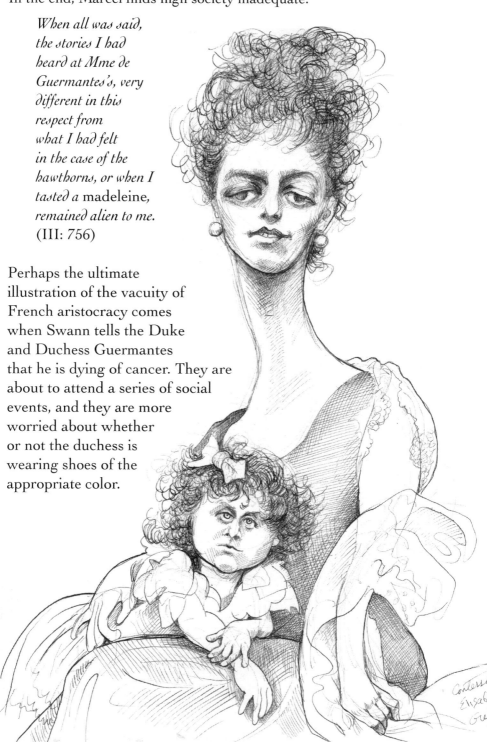

*When all was said,
the stories I had
heard at Mme de
Guermantes's, very
different in this
respect from
what I had felt
in the case of the
hawthorns, or when I
tasted a* madeleine,
remained alien to me.
(III: 756)

Perhaps the ultimate
illustration of the vacuity of
French aristocracy comes
when Swann tells the Duke
and Duchess Guermantes
that he is dying of cancer. They are
about to attend a series of social
events, and they are more
worried about whether
or not the duchess is
wearing shoes of the
appropriate color.

Temptation of St. Anthony
by Martin Schoengauer, circa 1470

90

Sodom and Gomorrah

Sodome et Gomorrhe

Sodom and Gomorrah (later Moncrieff)

Sodom and Gomorrah (Penguin)

The Cities of the Plain (early Moncrieff)

Sodom and Gomorrha

YEAR: 1899, Narrator about 19 years old

Only in succeeding volumes does the work become almost good....

— Proust, letter, September 15–16, 1920

A S ANDRÉ GIDE OBSERVED and as Proust himself might have conceded, during the first thirty years of his life, he was something of a twit. To a degree, this is reflected in the Narrator Marcel, who often seems sentimental, naive, and a dweeb. However, much as Marcel Proust matured, so in the fourth volume of RECHERCHE Marcel Narrator begins to see a world in richer, deeper, darker hues.

In the Hebrew Bible, Sodom and Gomorrah were cities located on the plain of Jordan that God destroyed by fire and brimstone because their inhabitants were irredeemably wicked.

> *Behold, this was the iniquity of thy sister Sodom, pride, fullness of bread, and abundance of idleness was in her and in her daughters, neither did she strengthen the hand of the poor and needy.*
> — Ezekiel 16:49

Because the rich never like to have attention called to their selfishness, of course, the sin of Sodom and Gomorrah has often been understood as the "sin" of homosexuality—a major theme of RECHERCHE's fourth volume.

Proust opens *Sodom and Gomorrah* with a quotation from the French writer Alfred de Vigny:

The women shall have Gomorrah
and the men shall have Sodom.

HE BEGINS WITH A FOCUS ON MEN, as Marcel watches Charlus and Jupien performing a mating dance before having relations. Eventually Charlus focuses his lust on Charlie Morel, the son of Marcel's uncle's valet. Morel is a professional violinist who likes men, little girls, and sometimes women. At one point, Morel is set to have a sexual encounter with Prince Guermantes, which Charlus and Jupien hope to watch.

For the time being, Saint-Loup has remained heterosexual, dumping Rachel for houses of prostitution and shifting his allegiance to the anti-Dreyfus side. One section of *Sodom and Gomorrah* takes the title *Intermittences of the Heart*, which Proust originally intended for all of *RECHERCHE*. Indeed the term does not apply only to Charlus and his adventures.

The primary model for Charlus, Robert de Montesqueou, proudly exhibiting his prize pedigree cats.

Right:
Ladies of the night awaiting Saint-Loup

Albertine has returned to Marcel's life now, and his emotions concerning her echo those of Swann and Odette and of himself and Gilberte, yet raise them to new levels. Marcel worries that Albertine has lesbian tendencies.

In doing so, Marcel echoes Thomas Hardy:

> *I am inclined to believe that in these relationships ... beneath the outward appearance of the woman, it is to those invisible forces with which she is incidentally accompanied that we address ourselves as to obscure deities. ... The woman herself, during our assignation with her, does little more than put us in touch with these goddesses.* (IV: 719)

At one point Marcel states, "The idea of marrying Albertine appeared to me madness." (IV: 698)

Yet by the end of the volume, he tells his mother, "I absolutely must marry Albertine." (IV: 724)

Sodom and Gomorrah also happens to contain what may be Proust's—or all of literature's—longest single sentence. In the Modern Library edition, it begins on page 21 ("Their honour precarious, their liberty provisional ...") and ends on page 24 ("... composed exclusively of persons similar to themselves."). The translation runs 958 words.

Marcel again finds himself shaken by memory association. Taking off his boots one day triggers a recollection of his dead grandmother, and he is overwhelmed with pain.

[M]y chest swelled, filled with an unknown, a divine presence, I was shaken with sobs, tears streamed from my eyes. ... I had just perceived, in my memory ... my grandmother.... (IV: 210)

And so ends our brief look at Sodom & Gomorrah

GENESIS 19 FROM GUSTAVE DORÉ'S ILLUSTRATED BIBLE, 1866

Proust's real-life cuddly, wayward chauffeur-secretary Alfred Agostinelli was reincarnated as Albertine after he flew an airplane into the sea—. to be trapped in Marcel's possessive obsession all over again.

R.I.P.

help!

THE CAPTIVE AND THE FUGITIVE

La Prisonnière	*Albertine disparue*
The Captive (later Moncrieff)	*The Fugitive* (later Moncrieff)
The Prisoner (Penguin)	*The Fugitive* (Penguin)
The Captive (early Moncrieff)	*The Sweet Cheat Gone* (early Moncrieff)
Die Gefangene	*Die Fluechtige*
YEAR: 1900	YEAR: 1901
Narrator about 20 years old	Narrator about 21 years old

*T*HE CAPTIVE/PRISONER AND *THE FUGITIVE* are usually packaged in two separate books in French and German; English editions typically combine them in one volume. The focus of both is Albertine.

The first book focuses on Marcel Narrator, his crazed jealousy, and his effort to control and contain his love. To no avail, he had been "warned" earlier by Swann:

> *The danger of that kind of love, however, is that the woman's subjection calms the man's jealousy for a time but also makes it more exacting. After a while he will force his mistress to live like one of those prisoners whose cells are kept lighted day and night to prevent their escaping. And that generally ends in trouble.* (II:188)

Not surprisingly, Albertine reacts to Marcel's control-freaking by running away. A greater surprise, after no small amount of drama and confusion, is that her flight ends in death.

THE WORLD OF SEX, meanwhile, grows more glittering and gruesome.

CHARLUS tries to arrange a marriage between the niece of his protégé, Jupien, and his protégé, Morel. Morel finds the proposition interesting because of the women the niece might procure for Morel and the "rich and beautiful ladies to whom he would prostitute" the niece.

Marcel, for his part, worries about whether Albertine appreciates anal sex and proceeds to grill her about it.

HE ALSO pays a little girl 500 francs to sit on his lap and gets hauled into court by her parents. The magistrate berates Marcel but, after the parents leave, reveals his own weakness for little girls. He "changed his tone and admonished me as man to man: 'Next time, you must be more careful. Good God, you can't pick them up as easily as that, or you'll get into trouble. Anyhow, you'll find dozens of little girls who are better-looking than that one, and far cheaper.'"
(V: 598–599)

Later, Marcel questions a friend of Albertine named Andrée about her sexual history. He learns about Albertine's lesbianism and her adventures with Morel. He hires two laundresses to make love in his presence

so he can get a better sense of Albertine's sexuality, and he makes love to Andrée in order to have sex with someone who has had sex with Albertine.

Gilberte, for her part, has become a rich heiress, and, thanks to Odette's third marriage, no longer has to worry about her Jewish surname. Gilberte's engagement with Robert Saint-Loup is announced, but Saint-Loup flaunts mistresses to cover his homosexual pursuits, including love letters with Morel.

M ORE SPIRITUAL AND PERHAPS MORE ENCOURAGING EPISODES are provided by the death of the novelist Bergotte and by a concert that Marcel attends with Albertine. Bergotte dies while examining Vermeer's *View of Delft*, with its singular patch of yellow.

> *[T]here is no reason inherent in the conditions of life on this earth that can make us consider ourselves obliged to do good, to be kind and thought- ful, even to be polite, nor for an artist to consider himself obliged to begin again a score of times a piece of work.... [T]hese obligations, which have no sanction in our present life, seem to belong to a different world, a world based on kindness, scrupulousness, self-sacrifice, a world entirely different form this one and which we leave in order to be born on this earth....* (V: 245–246)

Right: Proust based Bergotte on Anatole France and various other authors, including himself.
Above: Proust's last daytime outing, was to see Vermeer's **View of Delft**. He fell ill at the exhibition, then turned his experience into the death of Bergotte.

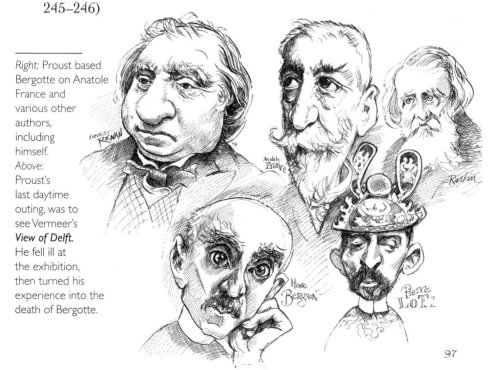

THE CONCERT MARCEL ATTENDS features a septet by a fictitious composer named Vinteuil, with Morel playing the star role as violinist. (Charlus' pathetic machinations in the concert constitute a comedy in their own right.) Vinteuil's music precipitates a number of thoughts and associations in Marcel:

I wondered whether music might not be the unique example of what might have been ... the means of communication between souls. It is like a possibility that has come to nothing; humanity has developed along other lines, those of spoken and written language. But this return to the unanalyzed was so intoxicating that, on emerging from that paradise, contact with more or less intelligent people seemed to me of an extraordinary insignificance. (V: 344)

Debussy

Franck

Saint-Saëns

It is inconceivable that a piece of sculpture or a piece of music which gives us an emotion that we feel to be more exalted, more pure, more true, does not correspond to some definite spiritual reality, or life would be meaningless. Thus nothing resembled more closely than some such phrase of Vinteuil the peculiar pleasure which I had felt at certain moments in my life, when gazing, for instance, at the steeples of Martinville, or at certain trees along a road near Balbec, or, more simply, at the beginning of this book, when I tasted a certain cup of tea.

(V: 504–505)

Fauré

Hahn

Proust's conception of Vinteuil's music evolved from Saint-Saens' "little phrase" as he worked on RECHERCHE, influenced by Debussy, Franck, Fauré, Wagner, and his friend Hahn.

Wagner

Beethoven death mask

Time Regained

Le Temps Retrouvé

Time Regained (later Moncrieff) • *Finding Time Again* (Penguin) • *The Past Recaptured*
(early Moncrieff) • *Die wiedergefundene Zeit* • Years: 1912–1919, Narrator 22 to pushing 40

WE WILL REFER TO *RECHERCHE*'S FINAL VOLUME AS LTR, for *Le Temps Retrouvé* (*Time Recovered*, or *Time Regained*, or *Finding Time Again*).

LTR IS WHERE EVERYTHING COMES TOGETHER AND IS EXPLAINED — which is one reason why a reader of *RECHERCHE* might want to begin with it. After all, given the circular structure of the full work, everything in Volume I (and all subsequent volumes) immediately follows the end of LTR.

> *[T]he last page of* Le Temps retrouvé *(written before the rest of the book) comes full circle to meet the first page of* Swann.
> — Proust, letter, January 18-19, 1922

For those interested in how Proust's novel echoes other works of literature, it might be observed that one section of LTR constitutes a single extended scene of discovery and recognition, much as in Sophocles' *Oedipus Rex*. The philosophical discussion that follows this elongated epiphany calls to mind the philosophical disquisitions contained in such 19th century novels as Victor Hugo's *Les Misérables*, Harriet Beecher Stowe's *Uncle Tom's Cabin*, Leo Tolstoy's *War and Peace*.

> *[O]nce people have finished the book they will see (I hope) that the whole novel is simply the implementation of the artistic principles expressed in this final part, a sort of preface if you like placed at the end.*
> — Proust, letter, August 1909

LTR begins with a sense of the-darkest-hour-before-the-dawn, followed by an explosion of dawn at the middle, and a final confrontation with the dark by the end.

It is around 1912. Marcel Narrator is visiting Gilberte, now the Marquise de Saint-Loup. Things are glum. Husband Robert, instead of being content with his "inversion," works at making his wife "ill with jealousy by keeping with mistresses without pleasure to himself." (VI: 20–21). From Gilberte, Marcel learns that he misread a signal from her many years ago which "would perhaps have changed the whole course of my life." (VI: 6). He learns that the "ways" of Swann and Guermantes "were not as irreconcilable as I had supposed." (VI: 40) Concluding that he has "no gift for literature," he renounces writing and, in deteriorating health, retreats to a sanatorium.

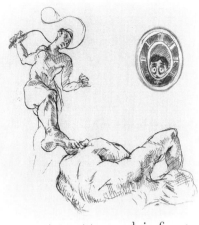

Marcel spends most of the period 1912–1919 in the sanatorium, except for a brief consultation in Paris in August 1914 and a more eventful visit there in 1916. On the latter trip, he finds himself in a brothel where, through a peephole, he watches a man being beaten with a studded whip by a rough sailor type. Later this customer discusses the quality of his experience with the brothel keeper: "I did not want to speak in front of that boy, who is very nice and does his best. But I don't find him sufficiently brutal. He has a charming face, but when he calls me a filthy brute he might be just repeating a lesson." (VI: 184) The customer in question turns out to be Baron Charlus, who bought the brothel for its present proprietor, Jupien. Marcel concludes that Charlus' "desire to be bound in chains and beaten, with all its ugliness, betrayed a dream as poetical as, in other men, the longing to go to Venice or to keep ballet-dancers." (VI: 218)

Marcel returns to another sanitarium, which proves "no more successful in curing me than the first one, and many years passed before I came away." (VI: 238) By this time, around 1919, Marcel's disillusionments have extended to his most central concern—becoming a writer:

During the train journey which eventually took me back to Paris, the thought of lack of talent for literature ... struck me afresh and with a force more painful than ever before." The train stops in open country where the sunlight shines on the trees. 'Trees,' I thought, 'you no longer have anything to say to me.... If ever I thought of myself as a poet, I know now that I am not one.' (VI: 238)

Then, however, Marcel accepts an invitation to a musical reception given by the Prince de Guermantes, and a new dawn begins to break:

[I]t is sometimes just at the moment when we think that everything is lost that the intimation arrives which may save us; one has knocked at all the doors which lead nowhere, and then one stumbles without knowing it on the only door through which one can enter—which one might have sought in vain for a hundred years—and it opens of its own accord. (VI: 254–255)

The door that finally opens for Marcel is actually a number of doors, a number of epiphanies, a number of variations on his original madeleine moment. The first comes with Marcel tripping on some uneven paving stones in the Guermantes courtyard. The epiphany begins there:

But at the moment when, restoring my balance, I put my foot on a paving stone which was a bit lower than the one before it, all my discouragement vanished before the same happiness which at different points in my life before had been given me, the view of the trees which I had thought I had recognized in a drive around Balbec, the view of the steeples of Martinville, the taste of a madeleine dipped in tea, and all the other sensations that I have discussed, and which the last works of Vinteuil seem to have synthesized. Just at the moment where I had tasted the madeleine, all anxiety over the future, all intellectual doubt, was dissipated. ... The happiness which I had just felt was an effect truly identical to that which I felt when eating the madeleine. ... [A] deep azure intoxicated my eyes... (see VI: 255–256)

Marcel attempts to recapture the thrill by repeating his staggering movement. Although he fails to recover the rapture, he does realize that the original moment derived from an experience he had in Venice in the baptistery of St. Mark's. "But why," Marcel wonders, had the images of Combray (called to mind by the madeleine) and of Venice, "given me a joy which was like a certainty and which sufficed, without any other proof, to make death a matter of indifference to me?" (VI: 257)

As he ponders this question, a butler leads him to a sitting room where

a second intimation came to reinforce the one which had been given to me by the two uneven paving-stones and to exhort me to persevere in my task. A servant, trying unsuccessfully not to make a noise, chanced to knock a spoon against a plate and again the same species of happiness which had come to me from the uneven paving-stones poured into me.... (VI: 257)

Marcel then experiences another flashback, this one involving the view of trees he had once enjoyed from a railway car. Before he can evaluate the second intuition, yet another arrives as he wipes his mouth with a napkin given to him by a different butler:

[A] new vision of azure passed before my eyes.... [T]he napkin which I had used to wipe my mouth had precisely the same degree of stiffness and starchedness as the towel with which I had found it so awkward to dry my face as I stood in front of the window on the first day of my arrival at Balbec. (VI: 258–259)

Again "swelling with happiness," Marcel reports that

I forced myself to the task of seeing clearly and as quickly as possible into the nature of the identical pleasures which I had experienced three times in a few minutes, and then extracting/ extricating the lessons that might be pulled/extracted from them. ..In truth, the being in me which had relished that impression, relished what it had in common with something in both the past and present, something beyond time… This explained why my anxiety over the subject of my death had ceased at the moment where I had unconsciously recognized the taste of the little madeleine, because at that moment the being I had been was a being beyond time, and, consequently, indifferent to the vicissitudes of the future. …at the time I had such an appetite to live…. (see VI: 259, 262, 263)

Marcel concludes that he has been experiencing "a fragment of time in the pure state," "nourished only by the essence of things." (VI: 264) "[T]he three memories ... instead of giving me a more flattering idea of myself, had almost caused me to doubt the reality, the existence of that self." (VI: 265)

He then hears water running through a pipe and experiences yet another, fourth, resurrection, where the past scene wrestles with the present surroundings.

Always the present scene had come off victorious, and always the vanquished one had appeared to me the more beautiful of the two, so beautiful that I had remained in a state of ecstasy on the uneven paving stones of before the cup of tea. ... [I]f the present scene had not very quickly been victorious I should have lost consciousness. (VI: 267)

The Guermantes Party

FRANÇOIS LE CHAMPI

These "[f]ragments of existence withdrawn from Time," Marcel declares, constitute "the only genuine and fruitful pleasure that I had known." (VI: 268) Accordingly,

> to this contemplation of the essence of things I had decided therefore that in the future I must attach myself, so as somehow to immobilize it. But how...? The only way to savour them more fully was to try to get to know them more completely in the medium in which they existed, that is to say within myself. (VI: 269, 271)

Marcel—both the Narrator and Proust—concludes that these explorations of self should be translated into art:

> For the truths which the intellect seizes directly... have something less profound, less necessary than that which life communicates to us in spite of ourselves. In fact, in one case as in another, whether the impression was produced by the sight of the steeples of Martinville, or the recollection of those uneven two steps, or the taste of the madeleine, the task came to

interpreting these sensations as signs of so many laws and ideas … to convert it into a spiritual equivalent. And this process, which seemed to me to be the only option, what could it be except to create a work of art? (see VI: 273)

A musical piece is already being performed at the Guermantes reception, so Marcel must wait in the library until its conclusion before being admitted. In the library, he happens upon the book his mother read to him in Volume I, George Sand's *François le Champi* — and he experiences his fifth and final epiphany:

> *I found myself unpleasantly struck by an impression which seemed at first to be utterly out of harmony with the thoughts that were passing through my mind, until a moment later, with an emotion so strong that tears came to my eyes, I recognized how very much in harmony with them it was…. The memory of what had seemed to me too deep for understanding in the subject of* François le Champi *when my mother long ago had read the book aloud to me, had been reawakened by the title ….* (VI: 281–283)

Marcel draws his own conclusions:

> *[T]he essential, the only true book … in the ordinary sense of the word does not have to be "invented" by a great writer — for it exists already in each of us…. The function and the task of a writer are those of a translator. … The work of art [is] the sole means of rediscovering Lost Time.* (VI: 291, 304)

Marcel summarizes his philosophy, echoing Plato's argument that what we regard as reality is actually shadows dancing on cave walls; the real reality lies behind that:

> *The greatness of true art … makes us recover, regain, and perceive that reality far from our daily living, from which we separate ourselves more and more, as the conventional knowledge which we substitute for it grows thicker and more impermeable, this reality which we are in danger of dying without having known it, and which, is, quite simply, our life…. This work of the artist, the search to perceive under matter, under experience, under words, something which is different, this work is exactly opposite to that effectuated in us minute by minute when we live diverted from ourselves by vanity, passion, intelligence, and habit too, when these classification, these practical goals, pile over our true impressions so as to hide them from us completely — and we falsely call that life…. The work done by our vanity, our passion, our spirit of imitation, our abstract intelligence, our habits, it is that work which art must destroy….* (see VI: 298–300)

Or, as he wrote more concisely in *Against Sainte-Beuve:*

What we are doing is making our way back to life, shattering with all our force the ice of the habitual and the rational which instantly congeals over reality and keeps us from ever seeing it. (267)

All that said, it is one thing to *think* about transcending Time and overcoming death. It is quite another to *live* it in practice. Marcel's newly won theories are put immediately to the test by the "reality" that includes the passage of time, deterioration, degeneration, and death. At this point in the novel, he is finally admitted to the Guermantes party. He refers to the experience as a puppet-show," or "theatrical pageant." It might as well be called a Dance of Death. For here Marcel and his readers confront the various characters they have come to know through the earlier volumes of RECHERCHE—except now it is 20 years later.

Gilberte
(stout)

A review of some of the characters already discussed provides a sense of the challenge that Marcel faces:

☞ His early girlfriend Gilberte has become so "stout" that she has to identify herself to Marcel before he recognizes her.

Saint Loup
(heroic, dead)

☞ Her husband Robert Saint-Loup has died a hero's death at the front.

☞ Saint-Loup's earlier mistress, Rachel, is now a "horrible old woman" but a famous actress, invited to recite poetry at the reception.

Rachel

☞ Rachel receives compliments from Bloch, now writing under the name Jacques du Rozier and affecting English ways; Marcel finds Bloch's works "absurd" and "without originality," yet he is now respected as a "great man."

☞ Saint-Loup's other main partner in sex, Charlie Morel, has been arrested as a deserter; returned to the front, he earns a decoration for bravery; by the time of the reception, he has become a respected public figure.

Charlie Morel

Saint-Loup's uncle Charlus has been reduced by strokes to a pathetic wreck (whom Marcel compares to King Lear).

Jupien now cares for Charlus: "I must not leave my invalid alone for a second, he is really just a big baby now." (VI: 245–253)

Charlus' cousin, the Prince de Guermantes, now "drag[s] his feet along the ground as though they were weighted with soles of lead." (VI: 336)

Prince Guermantes now has a new Princess, the insufferable Mme. Verduin.

The once witty and enchanting Duchesse (Oriane) Guermantes now affords newcomers the following impression: "What a stupid woman this is!" (VI: 464–465)

🐚 Duke de Guermantes, "as majestic and handsome as ever," "a magnificent ruin," (VI: 468, 483) now spends his time with

🐚 Odette, who, ironically, may remain the one character constant not only in her inconstancy, but also in her beauty, which "defies the laws of chronology." (VI: 377, 488)

This circus of degeneration and decrepitude simply underscores the significance of Marcel's insight. His experience has been a world of unrelenting instability, confusion, corruption, and betrayals. Yet his key discovery is that life does contain something solid, something dependable—indeed something so wonderful that one grows grateful for life; moreover, one loses one's fear of death. That "something" is Marcel's Time, a place (!) where the many aspects of experience—including its changes—remain and hang together. To grasp this is to experience ecstasy so profound that the rapture trumps everything. With this insight, Marcel can now sit down and write his book, the purpose of which will be to explicate this insight:

Odette

[I]t was time to begin if I wished to attain to what I had sometimes perceived in the course of my life, in brief lightning-flashes ... at those moments of perception which had made me think that life was worth living. How much more worth living did it appear to me now, now that I seemed to see that this life that we live in half-darkness can be illumined, this life that at every moment we distort can be restored to its true pristine shape, that a life, in short, can be realized within the confines of a book! (VI: 507)

LTR concludes with some symbolic instances of time resurrecting itself, such as recollections of Swann, without whom Marcel would never have gotten "the raw material for my book." (VI: 328) At the reception, Gilberte introduces Marcel to her daughter, also the daughter of Saint-Loup and granddaughter of Odette and Swann—a merging and "prolongation" of the Swann and Guermantes Ways, herself a materialization of Time.

In the final pages of LTR, Marcel recalls Albertine sleeping along with the noise of the garden bell at Combray. He realizes that Time "was my life, was in fact me, but also that I was compelled so long as I was alive to keep it attached to me." (VI: 531) The novel ends with a characteristically Proustian sentence, capped by the most Proustian of all words.

> *So, if I were given long enough to accomplish my work, I should not fail, even if the effect were to make them resemble monsters, to describe men as occupying so considerable a place, compared with the restricted place which is reserved for them in space, a place on the contrary prolonged past measure, for, simultaneously, like giants plunged into the years, they touch the distant epochs through which they have lived, between which so many days have come to range themselves—in Time.* (VI: 531–532)

At this point, presumably, Marcel sits down to write page one of Volume I.

> *It is indeed too little understood that my books form a structure, but the compasses being opened wide, the composition, which is rigorous, and to which all else is sacrificed, takes some time to discern. Although nobody will be able to deny it, once the last page of* Le Temps retrouvé *(written before the rest of the book) comes full circle to meet the first page of* Swann.
> —Proust, letter, January 18–19, 1922

*V*OILÀ OUR SYNOPSIS of *RECHERCHE*. We would like to have included more discussion of other characters—such as Mme. Villeparisis, or Francoise the cook, or Legardin the snob, or Aimé the waiter, or Norpois the diplomat, or the shallow Cambremers, to name just a few. And we would like to have discussed more plots, twists, turns, and coincidences—there are so many to choose from…

Any discussion of Proust poses the problem of where to stop between "How I became a writer" and repeating the novel in its entirety. The many literary critics who have written about Proust and *RECHERCHE* have made some very different decisions about what merits discussion. For example, Terence Kilmartin lists some 350 characters over the course of some 80 pages, Patrick Alexander identifies 60 main character in 130 pages, and Philippe Michel-Thiriet names almost 250 in 60 pages.

HMMMM.

IF, IN ORDER TO GIVE SOME ONE who had not read him an idea of what Proust is all about, we were to begin by enumerating his subjects —a holiday in his old village, Swann's love affair, the emotions of a little boy and girl playing in the gardens on the Champs-Elysées, a summer holiday on the Normandy coast in a luxury hotel facing the fluctuating waves of the sea, against which, gliding like Nereids, the faces of blossoming girls are picked out, etc. —we would immediately understand that such a list leads nowhere and that these subjects, that have been treated by thousands of times by novelists, do not suffice to define what Proust brings us.

—**José Ortega y Gasset**,
Spanish philosopher

For Kilmartin, the following themes are noteworthy:

AIRPLANES; ALCOHOL; AMERICANS; ANTI-SEMITISM; APPLE-TREES; AQUARIUM; ARABIAN NIGHTS; ART; ASPARAGUS;

BALLET; BEAUTY; BELIEF; BICYCLES; BIRDS; BODY; BRITISH; BROTHELS;

CLASS; DEATH; DOCTORS; DREAMS; DRESS; DREYFUS CASE; DRINK;

ENGLISH, ENGLISHMEN; FAUBOURG SAINT-GERMAIN; FLOWERS; FOOD; FRIENDSHIP;

FURNITURE; GAMES; GERMAN, GERMANS; HABIT; HAWTHORN; HEREDITY; HISTORY;

HOMOSEXUALITY; INTOXICATION; INVERSION; JEALOUSY; JEWS; LANGUAGE; LETTERS;

...as well as: LIFTS; LITERATURE; LOVE; LYING; MARRIAGE; MEDICINE; MEMORY; MONOCLES; MOON; MOTOR-CARS; MUSIC; NAMES; OLD AGE; PAINTING; PARTIES; PHOTOGRAPHY; POLITICS; RAILWAYS; ROOMS; SADISM; SEA; SERVANTS; SOLITUDE; SPEECH; STOCK EXCHANGE; SUN; TEARS; TELEPHONE; THEATRE; TIME; TRAINS; TREES; TRUTH; VICE; VIRTUE; WAR; WEATHER.

For Michel-Thiriet, principal themes include:

SNOBBERY; THE SALONS; THE "CERCLES"; SERVANTS; SOCIAL RELATIONSHIPS; LOVE; MEMORY AND OBLIVION; ILLNESS AND DEATH; RELIGION; ART (RUSKIN, VERMEER, RENOIR, MOREAU); MUSIC, LITERATURE; POLITICS; THE DREYFUS AFFAIR; JEWISHNESS; THE FIRST WORLD WAR.

Alexander lists no themes, but we will take this opportunity to note

FIVE THEMES FOR WHICH PROUST HAS BECOME FAMOUS:

☞ ASSOCIATIONAL PSYCHOLOGY: The mind can order things according to different principles, for example, logic or story. There is another system based on association which may appear random but which nevertheless entails its own rationality. During the 18th century, David Hume explored this concept in philosophy, and Laurence Sterne practiced it in his novel *Tristram Shandy*. By 1900, the relevance of this sort of associationalism to psychology was reviving, as William James talked about "streams of consciousness" and Freud wondered whether a cigar is really just a cigar — or a penis. Mark Twain used it to guide his autobiographical writing. The associations that objects precipitate constitute a key to Proust's novel, whose narrative follows paths of association as much as it does a rigorous plot line. If Proust did not inspire the efforts (and appreciation) of modernist writers like James Joyce and Virginia Woolf, he certainly reinforced appreciation of them.

Bust of Laurence Sterne (1713-1768) in Shandy Hall, Coxwold. Joseph Nollekens, sculptor

CHILDHOOD: As a topic worthy of literary consideration, childhood had been explored by Jean-Jacques Rousseau in *Émile* and George Eliot in *Mill on the Floss*. Proust took these concerns to new depth and sensitivity, inspiring German philosopher Walter Benjamin to investigate and write about his own childhood. Proust's pursuits paralleled those of Freud, who inspired everyone to explore if not appreciate his or her childhood.

DECLINE OF ARISTOCRACY: In an almost literal sense, the aristocracy of Europe began to slip off the world's stage over the course of Proust's lifetime. Proust documented the French version with a gimlet eye that suggested it was, in fact, time for them to go.

SITUATION OF HOMOSEXUALS IN SOCIETY: Proust's introduction and exploration of "inversion" is all but unprecedented in Western literature. In a sense, then, *RECHERCHE* marks the B.C. and A.D. for gay literature — B.C. standing for "Before Charlus," and A.D. for "After Doncières" (Doncières being where Charlus had one of his assignations with Morel.)

SITUATION OF JEWS IN SOCIETY: The attempt by Jews and Christians to associate and assimilate was a new phenomenon for 19th century Europe. Karl Marx commented in an essay titled "On the Jewish Question"; George Eliot made her literary contribution with *Daniel Deronda*. In *RECHERCHE*, Proust explored the experiences of Jews like Swann and Bloch, as well as the societal crisis precipitated by the Dreyfus Affair.

Above: J.-J. Rousseau from Houdon's sculpture in the Louvre.
Right: George Eliot, from a drawing by Frederick William Burton, 1864

Flux As Content

S MAY BE ALL TOO OBVIOUS to the reader, one of the major difficulties in summarizing Proust is that he is consciously amorphous—if not intentionally confusing—as a matter of both content and form.

As a matter of content, it is never entirely clear in *RECERCHE* what the present time is, let alone where past time has gone. Proust might have provided the dates of scenes and the age of the narrator (as Hachez tried to calculate), but he chose not to. In fact, not until the later Albertine volumes did he even mention that the narrator had a name. Thus, the reader is left with a sense that if one tries to pin things down with dates and named subjectivities, one is cheating or, more important, missing the point Proust is trying to make. Human experience is simply too multifaceted to be contained in a calendar or a birth certificate.

This is one reason why the notion of discussing Proust and plot seems so curious. Again, *RECERCHE*'s plot is simple to the point of silliness: "This is how I came to write." But if the "plot" that tries to bind the messy chaos of *RECERCHE* seems artificial, that in itself is part of Proust's point. Plots are tools that people use to contain and understand experience, but they are barely adequate—they do not comprehend anything.

THE CREATION OF COHERENT NARRATIVES IN THE BRAIN
is not limited to manipulation of low-level perception,
as occurs with visual saccades, but extends to higher
perceptual and cognitive levels. ... Confabulation ...
is not a process under voluntary control. Rather, it's
what the brain does when confronted with a problem
it cannot begin to solve: it makes a story from
whatever bits of experience it can dredge up, in much
in the same way that narrative dreams are created
from scraps of memory.

—David Linden, *The Accidental Mind*

CONSISTENT WITH THIS APPROACH, we have seen that Proust seldom presents a simplistic character. First impressions often prove wrong; indeed they are often intended to mislead. By the time he gives us the last impression of a character, we are hard-pressed to find anyone who is entirely consistent or coherent. Thus, for example, the Duchess Guermantes appears awesome at the beginning of *RECHERCHE* and empty at the end. Charlie Morel, apparently just a pervert and a deserter, is a talented violinist and a war hero.

Probably Proust is telling us that people simply are not simple. This is in keeping with his theme that the world is not simple. One fundamental way of sorting out the world is to begin with sex—certainly a common way of organizing things in many cultures and languages. It seems so natural. Yet Proust rejects sex as a means of comprehending the world because he has his doubts about the easy comprehensibility of the world. The world is chaotic, and so is sex. Saint-Loup, Charlus, and Albertine provide only three examples from *RECHERCHE* for whom sex explodes beyond the boundaries of gender, propriety, and rationality.

Nor does love help very much in sorting things out. In contrast to so many other novels, love in *RECHERCHE* affords limited to no redemption. The adventures of Swann, Charlus, Marcel, and many others characters attest to the fact that love is just crazy.

I F THE ESSENCE of modernity is change (because the essence of the Old Order was stability and tradition), then Proust may be the quintessential writer of modernity. Things change, people change, and nothing remains the same over time—unless one finds the Platonic world beyond Time.

CONSTANT REVOLUTIONIZING OF PRODUCTION, UNINTERRUPTED DISTURBANCE OF ALL SOCIAL CONDITIONS, EVERLASTING UNCERTAINTY AND AGITATION DISTINGUISH THE BOURGEOIS EPOCH FROM ALL EARLIER ONES ⌛ ALL FIXED, FAST-FROZEN RELATIONS, WITH THEIR TRAIN OF ANCIENT AND VENERABLE PREJUDICES AND OPINIONS, ARE SWEPT AWAY, ALL NEW-FORMED ONES BECOME ANTIQUATED BEFORE THEY CAN OSSIFY ⌛ ALL THAT IS SOLID MELTS INTO AIR, ALL THAT IS HOLY IS PROFANED, AND MAN IS AT LAST COMPELLED TO FACE WITH SOBER SENSES HIS REAL CONDITIONS OF LIFE, AND HIS RELATIONS WITH HIS KIND ⌛

—Karl Marx and Friedrich Engels, *The Communist Manifesto*

Flux As Form

I F THE WORLD SEEMS CHAOTIC, perhaps it is because our experiences of the world are chaotic. Often things come at us with no apparent logic, or in conflicting perceptions. Often we experience time as slow; other times it flies by. Humans try to impose order on experience with notions of cause and effect, neutral and consistent space and time, and comprehensible story lines. Philosophers such as Hume and Kant and Nietzsche have argued that such attempts are artificial, possibly dishonest, and probably desperate. Hence artists and philosophers have looked for alternative ways to (re)present the ways in which human experience is actually experienced.

WHAT A WEE LITTLE PART OF A PERSON'S LIFE ARE IN HIS ACTS AND WORDS! HIS REAL LIFE IS LED IN HIS HEAD....

— Mark Twain

P ROUST'S TACTIC OF A WANDERING FOCUS is an attempt to reflect the way humans really experience. One can always try to organize experience (or "reality") into chapters and according to dates — this helps understand Proust in one way. But if the chapters and dates seem artificial, it is because they are. And this is one of Proust's major points.

This feature — the difference between "time" and "duration": how long something takes by the clock and how long it seems while it is going on — is itself only one of the features of Proust's metaphysical picture. ... It is this play on the relativistic principle in the social and personal fields that gives Proust his philosophical interest and that makes his book, I suppose, the greatest philosophical novel ever written.

— Edmund Wilson

By his [Proust's] impressionism I mean his non-logical statement of phenomena in the order and exactitude of their perception, before they have been distorted into intelligibility in order to be forced into a chain of cause and effect.

—Samuel Beckett

How I would love to talk to you about Einstein! ... Apparently, our ways of distorting Time are analogous.

—Proust, letter, December 9–10, 1921

REALITY IS MERELY AN ILLUSION, ALBEIT A VERY PERSISTENT ONE

If a little dreaming is dangerous, the cure for it is not to dream less but to dream more, to dream all the time.

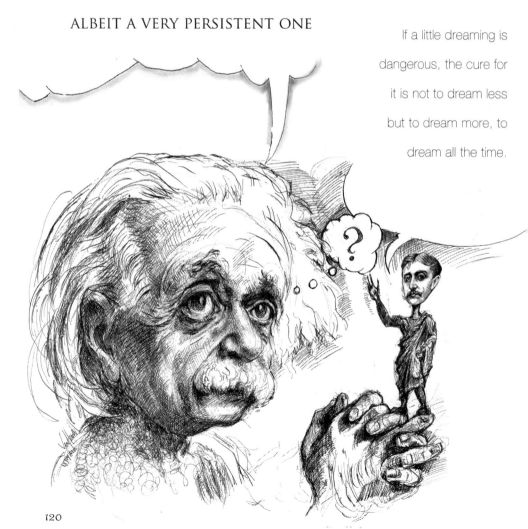

Those Long Sentences

I'm not trying to defend myself against the well-deserved reproach that my sentences are too often overlong, too closely intertwined with the meanderings of my thought....

— Proust, letter, May 11, 1921

OK, so Proust is trying to mime or re-present experience. The problem is that the experience he wants to recreate is one prior to or more basic than the "reality" humans create—and think they "really" inhabit—after they have processed the raw material of basic experience with arbitrary categories of cause, effect, time, space, etc. Proust is wandering and inclusive in the hope of capturing as much real reality as possible.

Proust's attempt to recapitulate this sense of reality goes down to the very building blocks of his novel—the sentences:

AN HOUR IS NOT MERELY AN HOUR, it is a vase full of scents and sounds and projects and climates, and what we call reality is a certain connection between these immediate sensations and the memories which envelop us simultaneously with them—a connection that is suppressed in a simple cinematographic vision, which just because it professes to confine itself to the truth in fact departs widely from it—a unique connection which the writer has to rediscover in order to link for ever in his phrase the two sets of phenomena which reality joins together.... (VI: 289)

121

PROUST FILLS HIS SENTENCES WITH SCENTS AND SOUNDS and projects and climates, immediate sensations, and memories, and then he tries to connect them. His sentences imitate his sense of how a human being really experiences a moment or an hour. Like his book, his sentences wander and ramble and include an extraordinary range of immediate sensations and distant thoughts. This method of presentation reflects Proust's sense of how reality is lived and how it should be depicted.

Fleeting, broken apart, and far-reaching, the Proustian sentence is the structure *of such intermittencies of the heart, whose meaning emanates from its form and content.*

—Julia Kristeva,
Bulgarian-French
philosopher

When the novelist Marcel Proust was still in the womb, his genteel mother was greatly distressed by the outbreak of the socialistic Paris Commune; and some speculate that this distress was the cause of Proust' lifelong asthmas. There is also a theory that Proust's immensely long sentences are a kind of psychological compensation for his breathlessness. In which case there is a relation between Proust's syntax and the Paris Commune.

—Terry Eagleton, English literary critic

People have tried to explain why his sentences are long; the explanation is very simply: they proustify incomparably....

—Fernand Gregh

In the end, Proust argues that his way of presenting reality presents a reality more real than the sort of writing that attempts only to re-present reality.

*T*HE REALITY THAT [THE WRITER] HAS TO EXPRESS *resides, as I now began to understand, not in the superficial appearances of his subject but at a depth at which that appearance matters little.... Nothing is further from what we have really perceived than the vision that the cinematograph presents.* (VI: 279)

WHATCHA SEE
IS WHATCHA GET:

The Credo of
Vulgar Materialism

*A*ND THIS *is why the kind of literature which contents itself with "describing things" is, in fact, though it calls itself realist, the furthest removed from reality and has more than any other the effect of saddening and impoverishing us, since it abruptly severs all communication of our present self both with the past, the essence of which is preserved in things, and with the future, in which things incite us to enjoy the essence of the past a second time. Yet it is precisely this essence that an art worthy of the name must seek to express....* (VI: 284)

THOSE STRUCTURED SENTENCES

Y ET EVEN AS HIS WORDS WANDER all over the page, there is one feature of many Proustian sentences that may be easy to miss but is important to recognize: they are often grounded in a conscious and conscientious structure.

One example is the sentence he uses to depict the discovery of Charlus as the paying "victim" in Jupien's brothel:

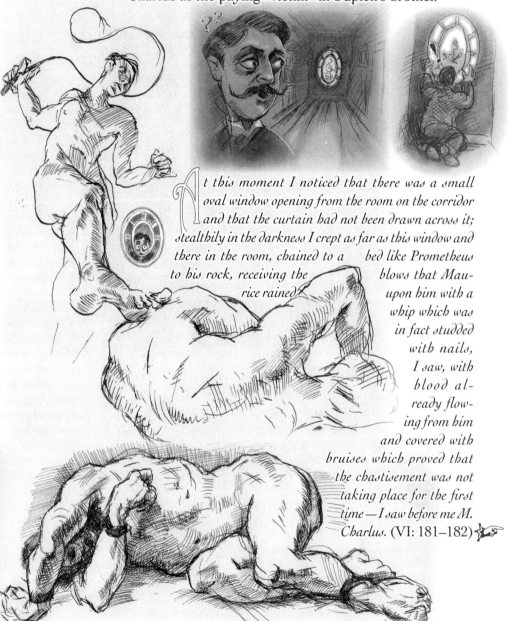

t this moment I noticed that there was a small oval window opening from the room on the corridor and that the curtain had not been drawn across it; stealthily in the darkness I crept as far as this window and there in the room, chained to a bed like Prometheus to his rock, receiving the blows that Mau-rice rained upon him with a whip which was in fact studded with nails, I saw, with blood already flowing from him and covered with bruises which proved that the chastisement was not taking place for the first time—I saw before me M. Charlus. (VI: 181–182)

... Monsieur Charlus!?!

NOTE HERE HOW THE SENTENCE HAS A BUILDUP, and how the buildup climaxes in the last word of the sentence—the revelation that it is the familiar Charlus in this unfamiliar, indeed shocking, setting. The end of the sentence serves as a climactic "pop" to the preceding phrases. It also serves as something of a summary of the entire sentence.

One contemporary critic has noted how this structuring tactic informs Proust's sentences:

> *[T]HE SENTENCE, as conceived—or as practiced— by Proust, was not only a vehicle for speaking his melancholy yearning for things that were, or never were, and might never be again; the sentence was also a medium for decrypting and unpacking, layer after layer, clause after clause, the Russian-doll universe that people turn out to be, Marcel included. The sentence is how Proust sees, or rather how he reveals, that universe. Revelation is key. Description is only interesting insofar as it leads to recognition and surprise.*

—André Aciman

By way of example in LTR,

> *I also thought of those who were not there, because they were unable, those whose secretaries, searching to give the illusion that they were surviving, had excused by one of those telegrams which from time to time were handed to the Princess, those invalids, dying for years, who never got up, never stirred, even in the middle of the frivolous attention of visitors drawn by a tourist's curiosity or a pilgrims' faith, their eyes closed, clutching their rosary, feebly pushing back the sheet which has already become a funeral shroud, are like monument effigies which illness has sculpted to a skeletal carcass, in a flesh rigid and white as marble, stretched over their tomb.*
> (see VI: 372)

In this description of people aging and dying, the sentence climaxes with, and is summarized by, the word "tomb" (*tombeau*). Many other Proustian sentences have such features.

PROUST AND PLATO

OF COURSE, if Proust's sentences try to tell us something about the nature of reality by their meanderings, so they tell us something about the nature of reality when they follow such conscientious structuring.

Again, Plato informs much of Proust. According to his view, there is fluttering chaos on the surface of perceived reality but something much more fundamental and ideal beyond it. Ordinary physical reality is ephemeral, temporary, and changing. The good stuff is everything permanent and perfect that lies underneath or within or beyond what we encounter initially. The ideal stuff is the real reality, while what we see in "normal" life is, at best, a reflection of something more fundamental.

FROM THE PLATONIC PERSPECTIVE, some of Proust's pronouncements begin to make more sense—even though they may still sound weird. For example, reality for Proust is much more spiritual/ideal/mental than it is material:

> *Dreams were another of the facts of my life which had always most profoundly impressed me and had done most to convince me of the purely mental character of reality....* (VI: 326–327)

He also has limited appreciation for the material, including human bodies:

> *Indeed, it is the possession of a body that is the great danger to the mind, to our human and thinking life, which it is surely less correct to describe as a miraculous entelechy of animal and physical life than as an imperfect essay....* (VI: 512)

And the reality of people more involves the divinities they reflect than the human beings they supposedly are. Remember Thomas Hardy?

> [E]very individual who makes us suffer can be attached by us to a divinity of which he or she is a mere fragmentary reflection, the lowest step in the ascent that leads to it, a divinity or an Idea which, if we turn to contemplate it, immediately gives us joy instead of the pain which we were feeling before —indeed the whole art of living is to make use of the individuals through whom we suffer as a step enabling us to draw nearer to the divine form which they reflect and thus joyously to people our life with divinities.... (VI: 303–304)

> [I]t is not to individuals that we should attach ourselves... it is not individuals who really exist and are, in consequence, capable of being expressed, but ideas. (VI: 318)

Thus, for Proust, love and lovers are of dubious value:

> Indeed I am inclined to believe that in these relationships, ... beneath the outward appearance of the woman, it is to those invisible forces with which she is incidentally accompanied that we address ourselves as to obscure deities. ... The woman herself, during our assignation with her, does little more than to put us in touch with these goddesses. ... Would we in fact go to so much trouble for the woman herself, if she were not complemented by these occult forces.... ? (IV: 719)

Likewise friendships and friends:

> The unreality of others is indicated ... [by] friendship, which is a simulacrum, since, for whatever moral reasons he may do it, the artist who gives up an hour of work for an hour of conversation with a friend knows that he is sacrificing a reality for something that does not exist (our friends being friends only in the light of an agreeable folly ... which at the bottom of our hearts we know to be no more reasonable than the delusion of the man who talks to the furniture because he believes that it is alive).... (VI: 268–269)

Ultimate Worth

Proust's sense about the way of the world raises the question of why it is worth reading him in the first place. The longer short summary of *Recherche* presented earlier runs as follows: "A guy who wants to write figures out something worth writing and writes about it." One shortcoming of this summary is that it says nothing about what the guy discovered. So what *did* he discover, and is it really worth writing about?

A summary of what Proust has discovered might be summarized as follows: Life appears to be a chaotic mess, but underneath its mundane features, one can find "real life," and it is there that one can ascertain life's meaning, as well as why one should bother with living through all the chaos and mess.

Recall Proust's long and short summaries of himself and his work:

> *The greatness of true art ... makes us recover, regain, and perceive that reality far from our daily living, from which we separate ourselves more and more, as the conventional knowledge which we substitute for it grows thicker and more impermeable, this reality which we are in danger of dying without having known it, and which, is, quite simply, our life.... This work of the artist, the search to perceive under matter, under experience, under words, something which is different, this work is exactly opposite to that effectuated in us minute by minute when we live diverted from ourselves by vanity, passion, intelligence, and habit too, when these classifications, these practical goals, pile over our true impressions so as to hide them from us completely—and we falsely call that life....* (see VI: 298–300)

> *What we are doing is making our way back to life, shattering with all our force the ice of the habitual and the rational which instantly congeals over reality and keeps us from ever seeing it....*" (Against Sainte-Beuve, 267)

A higher, more ideal reality does exists, but we have to get past the "ice" of our habituated patterns of living, and the role of art is to help us do that.

This insight is first revealed in Proust's madeleine moment, and the rest of Recherche involves Marcel's adventures in coming to re-experience and appreciate it. In fact, one might argue that pretty much everything that Proust has to say is contained in that madeleine moment, even if the rest of *Recherche* constitutes a detailed elaboration of those propositions.

Rather than explore how *Recherche* elaborates on the propositions, we will now focus on the madeleine moment itself. The reader can then proceed to the novel itself for all the succulent details, if s/he so desires.

Labeling the Madeleine Moment

Marcel learns through the course of *Recherche* that the shock of a "madeleine moment" is not unique to tasting a madeleine cake. It can be triggered by church steeples, the smell outside a public water closet, or a trio of trees. At the climax of *Recherche* in Volume VI (LTR), Marcel experiences five of them in a row, through five different stimuli: the stumble over an uneven paving stone, the sound of a spoon tapped against a plate, the sensation of a stiff napkin, the sound of water rushing through a pipe, and a book from a library.

RESURRECTION OF YOUNG PROUST
after Giulio Campagnola (1482?-1515?)
Metropolitan Museum of Art

The last five visitations—cobbles, spoon and plate, napkin, water in the pipes, and Françoise le Champi—*may be considered as forming a single annunciation and as providing the key to his life and work.* —Samuel Beckett

THUS THE MADELEINE MOMENT is a rare but fundamental feature of human experience. Does Proust give it a name?

Initially he seems to settle on the term "resurrection." He resorts to that label a number of times in *Recherche*.

Near the end of work, however, we find Proust also using the term "lighting flash":

ILLUMINATION OF YOUNG PROUST

... if I wished to attain to what I had sometimes perceived in the course of my life, in brief lightning-flashes ... at those moments of perception which had made me think that life was worth living. How much more worth living did it appear to me now, now that I seemed to see that this life that we live in half-darkness can be illumined.... (VI: 507)

AND IF AN ILLUMINATING "lightning flash" works as a label, so might "epiphany."

In the course of the Search, if the resonance-as-ecstasy appears as the ultimate goal of life, it is difficult to see what art can add to it, and the narrator suffers the greatest doubts about art. ... But at the end, we see what art is capable of adding to nature: it produces resonances themselves....

The entire interest thus shifts from the privileged natural moments to the artistic machine capable of producing or reproducing them, of multiplying them: the Book. In this regard, we can scarcely avoid the comparison with Joyce and his machine for producing epiphanies.

—GILLES DELEUZE, French philosopher

THE AMERICAN LITERARY CRITIC ROGER SHATTUCK called them "moments bienheureux" ("quite happy moments").

WALTER BENJAMIN adopted another term used by Proust (VI: 254), the word "door":

In Proust, too, we are guests who enter through a door underneath a suspended sign that sways in the breeze, a door behind which eternity and rapture await us.

SAMUEL BECKETT used the term "fetish." This label works at a mundane level because a fetish refers to something that inspires more than it is "supposed" to. (For example, a high-heel shoe has no intrinsic capacity for sexual arousal, yet it may inspire sexual arousal in a person who has a "fetish" for stiletto shoes.) The term "fetish" also works at a more elevated level, because a mundane object can also be used to inspire sacred sensations.

The source and point of departure of this "sacred action," the elements of communion, are provided by the physical world, by some immediate and fortuitous act of perception.

—Samuel Beckett

*M*any years had elapsed during which nothing of Combray, save what was comprised in the theatre and the drama of my going to bed there, had any existence for me, when one day in winter, as I came home, my mother, **seeing that I was cold, offered me some tea, a thing I did not ordinarily take. I declined at first, and then, for no particular reason, changed my mind.** [1] She sent out for one of those short, plump little cakes called "petites madeleines," [2] which look as though they had been moulded in the fluted scallop of a pilgrim's shell. [2] And soon, mechanically, weary after a dull day with the prospect of a depressing morrow, [1] I raised to my lips a spoonful of the tea in which I had soaked a morsel of the cake. No sooner had the warm liquid, and the crumbs with it, touched my palate than **a shudder ran through my whole body, and I stopped, intent upon the extraordinary changes that were taking place. An exquisite pleasure had invaded my senses,** [3] but individual, detached, with no suggestion of its origin. And at once the vicissitudes of life had become indifferent to me, its disasters innocuous, its brevity illusory — **this new sensation having had on me the effect which love has of filling me with a precious essence; or rather this essence was not in me, it was myself. I had ceased now to feel mediocre, accidental, mortal.** [4] Whence could it have come to me, this all-powerful joy? I was conscious that it was connected with the taste of tea and cake, but that it infinitely transcended those savours, could not, indeed, be of the same nature as theirs. Whence did it come? What did it signify? **How could I seize upon and define it?**

I drink a second mouthful, [5] in which I find nothing more than in the first, a third, which gives me rather less than the second. **It is time to stop; the potion is losing its magic.** [6] It is plain that the object of my quest, the truth, lies not in the cup but in myself. The tea has called up in me, but does not itself understand, and can only repeat indefinitely with a gradual loss of strength, the same testimony; which I, too, cannot interpret, though I hope at least to be able to call upon the tea for it again and to find it there presently, intact and at my disposal, for my final enlightenment. I put down my cup and **examine my own mind. It is for it to discover the truth. But how? What an abyss of uncertainty whenever the mind feels that some part of it has strayed beyond its own borders; when it, the seeker, is at once the dark region through which it must go seeking, where all its equipment will avail it nothing. Seek? More than that: create. It is face to face with something which does not so far exist, to which it alone can give reality and substance, which it alone can bring into the light of day.** [7] (1: 60–61)

The Madeleine Paragraph

Let us turn now to the famous paragraph in Proust's narrative that focuses on his encounter with the madeleine. As reproduced at left, **bold type** and **[numbers]** refer to characteristics of the resurrection experience discussed in the pages that follow.

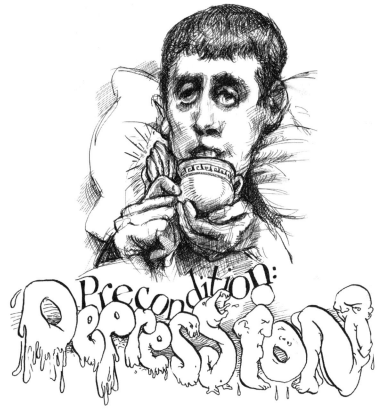

Precondition: Depression

[1] "[M]y mother, seeing that I was cold, offered me some tea, a thing I did not ordinarily take. I declined at first, and then, for no particular reason, changed my mind.... And soon, mechanically, weary after a dull day with the prospect of a depressing morrow...."

Roger Shattuck has pointed out that Proust's resurrections often seem to be preceded by a sense of physical, mental, or moral fatigue—or any combination of these. Thus, just before he encounters the madeleine, Marcel is not only cold but also "**weary after a dull day with the prospect**

of a depressing morrow." And just before his series of five climactic resurrections in LTR, he has all but given up on the hope of becoming a writer. In one of his earlier attempts at articulating the phenomenon of resurrection, Proust places his character Jean Santeuil in a state a "disappointment. His day had been completely, finally ruined." (*Jean Santeuil*, 406)

Why such a condition should constitute a precondition of a resurrection experience is suggested by Proust's discussion of such matters in the Preface to *Against Sainte-Beuve*.

> *And when the summer had passed, the sensation of this zwieback softened in the tea provided a refuge where the dead hours —dead to the intellect— went to nestle, and where I would, no doubt, never have recovered them, if that winter evening, returned frozen by the snow, my cook had not proposed that potion which was linked to that resurrection by virtue of a magic pact which I did not know.* (see 20)

Fatigue and despair help undermine the intellect; the analytical capacity is weakened (**"for no particular reason I changed my mind"**). Conscientious thinking can no longer stand in the way of other modalities of the brain to take in sensations and make "irrational" connections. The religious gloss here should also be acknowledged: one must be dead before one can be raised from the dead.

[2] She sent out for one of those short, plump little cakes called "petites madeleines," which look as though they had been moulded in the fluted scallop of a pilgrim's shell.

The reader will recall that, in the early draft (*Against Sainte-Beuve*), the madeleine took the form of a piece of dry toast. Why did Proust decide to change it to a madeleine in RECHERCHE? Aside from the suggestion that a madeleine cupcake might be more poetic than a shard of burnt bread, there is the matter of shape: madeleines "look as though they had been moulded in the fluted scallop of a pilgrim's shell."

St. James the Apostle coming ashore near Compostela

Some background helps here. Before Illiers/Combray became famous as a location in RECHERCHE, it had been known as a stopping point for religious pilgrims during the Middle Ages. In England, one might go on a pilgrimage to see St. Thomas Becket's bones in Canterbury. On the European continent, one of the major pilgrimage destinations was the shrine of St. James the Apostle at Compostela in northwestern Spain. James' shrine was located in Spain because, after the death of Jesus, he went there presumably to pave the way for the Apostle Paul's intended missionary work. In 40 A.D., however, the Virgin Mary appeared to James and told him to return to Judea; he did so and he died at the hands of King Herod. James' body was sent by ship to Spain, where the boat sank in the Atlantic Ocean, near Compostela.

There were many pilgrimage routes across Europe to Compostela, and Illiers stood on one of them. The scallop shell was a symbol associated with the route and those who took it, because James's body washed ashore in a protective layer of scallop shells. To the present day, pilgrims to Santiago de Compostela wear or carry pilgrim shells during their trek and bring them home as souvenirs as or proof that they have completed the pilgrimage. Scallop shells also serve as trails markers on many of the St. James routes. Thus, long before Illiers/Combray was selling scallop-shaped madeleines to Proust tourists, the town had been selling scallop-shaped madeleines to St. James pilgrims.

Thus it is entirely appropriate that Proust should allude to a pilgrim shell in his first experience of resurrection. The event marks the beginning of a long pilgrimage, RECHERCHE itself.

> [F]or me the novel is not only plane psychology but psychology in space and time. ... Then, like a city which, while the train pursues its winding course, seems to be first on our right, then on our left, the varying aspects the same character will have assumed to such a degree that they will have made him seem like successive and different character....
>
> —Proust, letter, November 1912

Any self-respecting pilgrimage will climax with its own religious overtones, often involving an effusion of light. Happily, the Spanish found the body of St. James because of an emanating light, comparable to the dazzle emanating from the angel(s) attending Jesus' empty tomb.

Presumably such light was similar to the light that attended Proust's own experiences of resurrection.

> I had not gone in search of the two uneven paving-stones of the courtyard upon which I had stumbled. But it was precisely the fortuitous and inevitable fashion in which this and the other sensations had been encountered that proved the trueness of the past which they brought back to life, of the images which they released, since we feel, with these sensations, the effort that they make to climb back towards the light, feel in ourselves the joy of rediscovering what is real. (VI: 272)

> [I]t was a time to begin if I wished to attain to what I had sometimes perceived in the course of my life, in brief lightning-flashes ... at those moments of perception which had made me think that life was worth living. How much more worth living did it appear to me now, now that I seemed to see that this life that we live in half-darkness can be illumined.... (VI: 507)

The final propriety is observed in the fact that it was Mary Magdalen (as in "madeleine") who was the first person to discover Jesus' resurrection:

> And, behold, there was a great earthquake: for the angel of the Lord descended from heaven, and came and rolled back the stone from the door, and sat upon it. His countenance was like lightning, and his raiment white as snow.
>
> —Matthew 28:2–3

> Now when Jesus was risen early the first day of the week he appeared first to Mary Magdalene, out of whom he had cast seven evils.
>
> —Mark 16:9

Mary stood without at the sepulcher weeping.... [S]he turned herself back, and saw Jesus standing, and knew not that it was Jesus. Jesus saith unto her, Woman, why weepest thou? She, supposing him to be the gardener, saith unto him, Sir, if thou have borne him hence, tell me where thou hast laid him, and I will take him away. Jesus saith unto her, Mary. She turned herself, and saith unto him, Rabboni; which is to say, Master. ...

—John 20:11,14–16

Did you ever hear, not of a Maud, but a Madeleine who went down to her garden in the dawn, and found One waiting at the gate, whom she supposed to be the gardener?

—John Ruskin, *Sesame and Lilies*

Thus the reader/pilgrim will travel through a number of volumes with Proust before finally reaching the destination of epiphany, where s/he will learn that life has meaning and death can be overcome.

And thus the madeleine— as opposed to a piece of dry toast—intimates a coming rapture. It is that aspect of the madeleine experience that we cover next.

[3] a shudder ran through my whole body, and I stopped, intent upon the extraordinary changes that were taking place. An exquisite pleasure had invaded my senses,

A madeleine moment (as a "resurrection" experience) can be identified by its exquisite, overwhelming joy. It entails rapture, ecstasy, communion with the divine. The language Proust uses to describe resurrections refers to something more than just a gentle turning on of lights:

☞ "At a bend in the road I experienced, suddenly, that special pleasure, which bore no resemblance to any other" (I: 253–254)

☞ "overpowered by a sort of intoxication, I could no longer think of anything but them" (I: 255)

☞ "filled me with a pleasure of a different kind from other pleasures, which leave one more unstable, incapable of grasping them, of possessing them, a pleasure that was solid and consistent, on which I could lean for support, delicious, soothing" (II: 88)

🖛 "suddenly I was overwhelmed with that profound happiness" (II: 404)

🖛 "touched to the heart" (II: 684)

🖛 "my chest swelled, filled with an unknown, a divine presence, I was shaken with sobs, tears streamed from my eyes" (IV: 210)

🖛 "I was favoured with ... a magical apparition" (V: 331)

🖛 "unknown country" (V: 342)

🖛 "with men like these we do really fly from star to star" (V: 343)

🖛 "I was truly like an angel ... fallen from the inebriating bliss of paradise" (V: 344)

🖛 "an ineffable joy which seemed to come from paradise. ... I knew that this new tone of joy, this summons to a supraterrestrial joy, was a thing that I would never forget." (V: 347)

🖛 "all my discouragement vanished and in its place was that same happiness which at various epochs of my life had been given to. ... The happiness which I had just felt was unquestionably the same as that which I had felt when I tasted the madeleine soaked in tea" (VI: 255–256)

🖛 "that same species of happiness which had come to me from the uneven paving-stones poured into me" (VI: 257–258)

🖛 "what I found myself enjoying was not merely these colours but a whole instant of my life on whose summit they rested ... now, freed from what is necessarily imperfect in external perception, pure and disembodied, caused me to swell with happiness. (VI: 258–259)

🖛 "so beautiful that I had remained in a state of ecstasy. ... And if the present scene had not very quickly been victorious, I believe that I should have lost consciousness ... the only genuine and fruitful pleasures that I had known" (VI: 266–268)

🖛 "an emotion so strong that tears came to my eyes" (VI: 281–283)

The mistake of philosophy is to presuppose within us a benevolence of thought, a natural love of truth. Thus philosophy arrives at only abstract truths that compromise no one and do not disturb. "The ideas formed by pure intelligence have only a logical truth, a possible truth, their election is arbitrary." [III: 880] ... They remain gratuitous because they are born of the intelligence that accord them only a possibility and not of a violence or of an encounter that would guarantee their authenticity.   ... There are few themes on which Proust insists as much as on this one: truth is never the product of a prior disposition but the result of a violence in thought.

—Gilles Deleuze, *Proust and Signs*

The concept of revelation—in the sense that suddenly, with indescribable certainty and subtlety, something becomes visible, audible, something that shakes one to the last depths and throws one down—that merely describes the facts. One hears, one does not seek; one accepts, one does not ask who gives; like lightning, a thought flashes up, with necessity, without hesitation regarding its form—I never had any choice.... Everything happens involuntarily in the highest degree but as in a gale of a feeling of freedom, of absoluteness, of power, of divinity . . . —Friedrich Nietzsche, *Ecce Homo*

The Sublime consists in a consummate excellence and distinction of language.... For the effect of genius is not to persuade the audience but rather to transport them out of themselves. ... A well-timed flash of sublimity shatters everything like a bolt of lightning. ... For the true sublime naturally elevates us. ... Sublimity lies in elevation, amplification rather in amount.

—Longinus, "On the Sublime"

[4] And at once the vicissitudes of life had become indifferent to me, its disasters innocuous, its brevity illusory—this new sensation having had on me the effect which love has of filling me with a precious essence; or rather this essence was not in me, it was myself. I had ceased now to feel mediocre, accidental, mortal.

The resurrection experience involves not only sensual joy, but also moral rapture. Life has meaning. One no longer fears death. And this is not a matter of intellectual argument. The resurrection by its very nature proves its "truths."

🖎 "a pleasure that was solid and consistent, on which I could lean for support, delicious, soothing, rich with a truth that was lasting, unexplained and sure" (II: 88)

🖎 "in attaching myself to the reality of that pleasure alone could I at length begin to lead a true life. . . Presently, at a cross-roads, the carriage left [the trees]. It was bearing me away from what alone I believed to be true, what would have made me truly happy; it was like my life" (II: 405, 407)

🖎 "I knew that this new tone of joy, this summons to a supraterrestrial joy … contrasting so sharply with all the rest of my life, with the visible world—those impressions which at remote intervals I experienced in my life as starting-points, foundation-stones for the construction of a true life" (V: 347)

🖎 "all anxiety about the future, all intellectual doubts had disappeared" (VI: 255)

🖎 "But why had the images of Combray and of Venice, given me a joy which was like a certainty and which sufficed, without any other proof, to make death a matter of indifference to me?" (VI: 257)

🖎 "This explained why it was that my anxiety on the subject of my death had ceased at the moment when I had unconsciously recognized the taste of the little madeleine" (VI: 262)

🖎 "even if the simple taste of a madeleine does not seem logically to contain within it the reasons for the joy, one can understand that the word "death" should have no meaning for him" (VI: 265)

🖎 "in brief lightning flashes … those moments of perception ... had made me think that life was worth living" (VI: 507)

🖎 "it would be the merest folly to be frightened of death. ... the thought of death had become a matter of indifference to me" (VI: 516)

Honest things, like honest men, do not carry their reasons in their hands like that. It is indecent to show all five fingers. What must first be proved is worth little. —Friedrich Nietzsche, *Twilight of the Idols*

[5] How could I seize upon and define it? I drink a second mouthful. . .

A resurrection is not something that can be turned on and off like a water faucet. It is not susceptible to intellectual manipulation or individual volition. Proust notes this characteristic when he shows that subsequent sips on the tea fail to rouse him as the first taste did. He emphasizes this point at two important junctures in the final volume of *Recherche*.

First, Marcel's climactic wave of resurrections begins when he trips on cobblestones in the Guermantes courtyard. He suddenly finds himself flooded with the happiness that attended his tasting of the madeleine. However, when he tries to repeat the rapture by repeating the stumble, he fails.

SIMILARLY, Charlus fails to reach ecstasy when he attempts to stimulate it with his sailor in the brothel. What may first appear to be an incident included for its salacious overtones is in fact an illustration not only of Charlus' character in particular, but also an illustration of the nature of resurrections in general. Charlus may be an "invert," and he may be attempting an invert's version of a resurrection, but the point about resurrections is that they cannot be consciously manufactured.

That this point is important to Proust is indicated by a change in verb tense during his account of the madeleine experience: Not "I drank a second mouthful," but "I drink a second mouthful." The shift in tense is something that French speakers often do in order to express significance. English speakers sometimes resort to this rhetorical technique, but not as frequently. (For example, "Well, I ran around, and I got to the outside—and suddenly Chris passes me the ball! I take it and I'm racing toward the goal!") This is a rhetorical tactic that can be traced back to classical times.

[I]f you introduce events in past time as happening at the present moment, the passage will be transformed from a narrative into a vivid

*actuality. "Someone has fallen," says Xenophon, "under Cyrus' horse and, as he is trodden under foot, is striking the horse's bellow with his dagger. The horse, rearing, throws Cyrus, and he falls." Thucydides uses such effects very ofte*n.

—Longinus, "On the Sublime"

The assertion that a resurrection can be experienced only in involuntary fashion has theological overtones: it is a matter of the grace of God, not of human effort.

However, the involuntary nature of the resurrection experience also held important secular implications for Proust. The involuntary nature of these experiences, he thought, attested to their scientific truth:

> *The impression is for the writer what experiment is for the scientist, with the difference that in the scientist the work of the intelligence precedes the experiment and in the writer it comes after the impression.... I had then arrived at the conclusion that in fashioning a work of art we are by no means free, that we do not choose how we shall make it but that it pre-exists us and therefore we are obliged, since it is both necessary and hidden ... to discover it.* (VI: 276–277)

For all of Proust's Catholic allusions, his "resurrections" went beyond religion; they were matters of science. As the son and brother of French doctors, Proust could resort to the rhetoric of science:

Indeed, it is the possession of a body that is the great danger to the mind, to our human and thinking life, which it is surely less correct to describe as a miraculous entelechy of animal and physical life than as an imperfect essay—as rudimentary in this sphere as the communal existence of protozoa attached to their polyparies or as the body of the whale—in the organization of the spiritual life. (VI: 512)

And he draws an analogy between the work of the artist and the work of the scientist.

At the beginning of the war M. Barres had said that the artist ... must first and foremost serve the glory of his country. But this he can do only by being an artist, which means only on condition that, while in his own sphere he is studying laws, conducting experiments, making discoveries which are as delicate as those of science, he shall think of nothing—not even his country—but the truth which is before him. (VI: 279–280)

This is one reason why we have referred to his work as RECHERCHE, and not SEARCH. The French language provides two word options: *cherche* and *recherche*, just as English provides search and research. Proust's RECHERCHE is a pilgrim's quest, and in that sense it is indeed a search or quest. But "quest" is only one translation of *recherche*; it can also be translated as "research" or "investigation." Proust's novel does in fact entail a rigorous investigation of scientific truth and, as such, resembles the work of Madam Curie and her groundbreaking 1905 essay, *Recherches sur les substances radioactives* ("Researches/ Investigations on radioactive substances").

Proust did not give his work the general title of *À la recherche du temps perdu* for nothing. Proust is indeed an investigator of lost time.

ORTEGA Y GASSET

[6] It is time to stop; the potion is losing its magic.

The negative water faucet analogy for the Proustian resurrection is apt not only because resurrections cannot be turned on and off at will. In addition, unlike water from water faucets, resurrections are not commonplace and appear only seldomly. Accordingly, they appear infrequently throughout the course of *RECHERCHE*. This is consistent with what Proust believed before writing his novel.

The stuff of our books, the substance of our sentences, should be drawn from our imagination, not taken just as it comes from real life; but our actual style, and the episodes too, should be made out of the transparent substance of our best moments, those in which we transcend reality and the present. It is from those consolidated drops of light that the style and the story of a book are made. (Against Sainte-Beuve, 273)

[The poet] gives up on looking for happiness except in the light of those rarefied moments which seem to him authentic existence. ("The Artist in Contemplation," 312)

In any case, though an ambitiously-minded man should feel an ideal love—even though his ambitious thoughts may not be transfigured by it—that love, alas! is not the whole of his life and often is no more than the few best days of his youth. It is with that part of himself alone that a writer composes his book.... (Against Sainte-Beuve, 160)

Ascertainment

[7] … examine my own mind. It is for it to discover the truth. But how? What an abyss of uncertainty whenever the mind feels that some part of it has strayed beyond its own borders; when it, the seeker, is at once the dark region through which it must go seeking, where all its equipment will avail it nothing. Seek? More than that: create. It is face to face with something which does not so far exist, to which it alone can give reality and substance, which it alone can bring into the light of day.

In this series of sentences, Proust sets out the terms of the struggles of his book. On the one hand, he learns that the resurrection experience is a door to rapture, and that rapture is a function of the Eternal space/time he has found. He refers to the resurrection experience as

- *"extra-temporal"*

- *"outside time"*

- *"a fragment of time in the pure state"*

- *"the essence of things"*

- *"freed from the order of time"*

- *"fragments of existence withdrawn from Time"*

But is it a matter of discovery only? While ascertaining Lost Time requires mental effort, another level of effort is required to comprehend it sufficiently to convey to it other people. This is the realm of Art and the task of the Artist. When the writer Proust articulates Lost Time, he recapitulates the experience not only for himself, but he makes it available to other people as well. And to make it available, he faces the challenge of finding and creating language that not only proves appropriate to the experience, but also does not revert to cliché.

Sainte-Beuve … did not ascertain that in literary work one sits in solitude, and one must work to suppress all the language that has been given to us from others, and even when we are alone we use those words to conceptualize things, and therefore lose our own true selves; literary work involves a confrontation between our superficial false, external and socialized self and our fundamental true internal individual self; and there one must strive to hear the true sounds from the inner heart, and express them in words which do not derive from society's overwhelming chatter. (Against Sainte-Beuve, see 103)

The result is not only a singular vision, but also a singular use of language to convey it.

Others may access rapture through their own openness to and explorations of their own experiences; and/or they may access it through the work of Proust and other artists.

I had made this discovery of this destructive action of Time at the very moment when I had conceived the ambition to make visible, to intellectualize in a work of art, realities that were outside Time. (VI: 351)

[A]t the end, we see what art is capable of adding to nature: it produces resonances themselves…. The entire interest thus shifts from the privileged natural moments to the artistic machine capable of producing or reproducing them, of multiplying them: the Book. In this regard, we can scarcely avoid the comparison with Joyce and his machine for producing epiphanies.

—Gilles Deleuze

THE TITLE AND ITS TRANSLATION—
A POINT FOR THE COCKTAIL PARTY

My English friends … [have] seen an announcement of my book with a title that means (I repeat it roughly) Souvenirs des choses pasées *instead of* À la recherche du temps perdu. *This ruins my title.* —Proust, letter, September 14, 1922

C.K. Scott-Moncrieff originally translated Proust's French title, *À la recherche du temps perdu*, as *Remembrance of Things Past*, alluding to Shakespeare's Sonnet 30. This upset Proust, in part because the double allusion of *temps perdu* was lost in translation. Proust appreciated that *temps perdu* could mean not only "time lost," but also "time wasted." Subsequently, *À la recherche du temps perdu* has been translated as *In Search of Lost Time;* in this study we have emphasized the research connotations of search/*recherche*.

Again, part of the reason why Proust insists that the findings of his research reveal objective truth is the fact that his findings have come to him involuntarily. They result from objective fact as opposed to subjective fancy. Hence, Proust had yet another reason to object to Scott-Moncrieff's allusion to Sonnet 30, which reads as follows:

> *When to the sessions of sweet silent thought*
> *I summon up remembrance of things past,*
> *I sigh the lack of many a thing I sought,*
> *And with old woes new wail my dear time's waste:*
> *Then can I drown an eye, unused to flow,*
> *For precious friends hid in death's dateless night,*
> *And weep afresh love's long since cancelled woe,*
> *And moan the expense of many a vanished sight:*
> *Then can I grieve at grievances foregone,*
> *And heavily from woe to woe tell o'er*
> *The sad account of fore-bemoanèd moan,*
> *Which I new pay as if not paid before.*
> *But if the while I think on thee, dear friend,*
> *All losses are restored and sorrows end.*

C.K. Scott-Moncrieff

In other words, while Shakespeare claims that the mind may, of its own accord, revive remembrances of things past, Proust alleges the opposite. For Proust, the revival of the past happens involuntarily, independent of the subject's will or actions. Again, this involuntary quality points to the truth of his findings. In the last volume of his novel, Proust is careful to emphasize this point. The cascade of his final epiphanies occurs involuntarily; only later can he attribute this to their objective, scientifically true existence.

Resurrection

Summary and Samples

IN SUM, that which has been called a "madeleine moment" can also be called a resurrection, a lightning flash, an epiphany, an extremely happy moment, a door, or a fetish.

SUCH PHENOMENA HAVE THE FOLLOWING FEATURES:

1. They tend to be preceded by physical, mental, or moral fatigue.

2. They can be stimulated by something as mundane as dry toast.

3. They involve physical ecstasy.

4. The rapture is so intense that one believes life is worth living, and one no longer fears death.

5. The raptures are involuntary; they come of their own accord and cannot be manufactured.

6. The experiences are rare; they don't come often.

7. The experiences point to an alternate reality, and part of the problem is perceiving that; another part is articulating what one perceives, and that involves effort in its own right, in terms of overcoming stale cliché and inventing new ways of putting words together.

So at this point one might want to seek out such an experience—or at least be open to it. Most likely one will NOT experience it by travelling to Illiers/Combray, buying a madeleine from a local baker, and munching on it, as some tourists do. To follow Proust, it is best to use him as a guide but not imitate him. In repetition lies failure, as Marcel would tell you after tripping on the cobblestones or Charlus would confirm after his encounter in the brothel. Nevertheless, the reader may be encouraged by knowing some of the stimuli that Proust identified in his writings:

the Outline of a church Steeple

the distant sound of an airplane

WASHROOM FROM WHICH ONE CAN LOOK TO THE SEA

- a road drying after rain
- earliest chills of coming winter
- the sound of a rubber tire
- the smell of a scrap of fabric
- the smell of a perfume
- light shining into one's room
- a level ray of the setting sun
- book binding
- breakfast coffee
- the sound of bells at noon
- mornings with the hiccups of central heating
- the distant sound of an airplane
- the outline of a church steeple
- the warbling of a thrush

WARBLING THRUSH

- the smell in a deplorable wooden villa at the seaside
- eating light-colored grapes
- the taste of dark, spiced stewed fruit, in hotel rooms with dusty furniture
- a bathroom with wet soap, eau-de-Cologne, mouthwash, and sunlight

- the smell of railway carriages
- the sound of limping, echoing bells
- the fragrance of roses

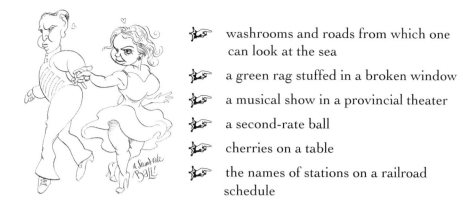

- washrooms and roads from which one can look at the sea
- a green rag stuffed in a broken window
- a musical show in a provincial theater
- a second-rate ball
- cherries on a table
- the names of stations on a railroad schedule

In addition to these, Proust might point to works of art for inspiration and guidance. When asked to pick eight masterpieces from the Louvre, he identified the following:

> *Portrait de lui-même* by Chardin, *Portrait de Mme Chardin* by Chardin, *Nature morte* by Chardin, *Le Printemps* by Millet, *Olympia* by Manet, *Les Falaises d'Étreat* by Monet…. A Renoir, or else *La Barque de Dante* or *La cathédrale de Chartres* by Corot. Either *L'Indifférent* by Watteau or his *L'Embarquement*.
>
> —Proust, letter February 1920

In the realm of music, one biographer reports that during the Great War, Proust especially appreciated the following works and sometimes hired the Poulet Quartet to play them for him privately:

- Beethoven's Twelfth Quartet
- Beethoven's Thirteenth Quartet
- Fauré's Quartet for Piano, Violin, Viola and Cellor No. q in C minor, Op. 15
- Franck's Quartet in D

Franck

Beethoven

Fauré

THE GOOD NEWS FOR ENGLISH SPEAKERS is that some of Proust's favorite works of literature need not even be read in translation.

> *It is curious that in all the different* genres, *from George Eliot to Hardy, from Stevenson to Emerson, there is no literature which has as much hold on me as English and American literature. Germany, Italy, very often France, leave me indifferent. But two pages of* Mill on the Floss *reduce me to tears.* —Proust, letter, December 1909

Can Proust Change Your Life?

Bad literature shrinks things.

—Proust, letter, September 1922

GOOD ART, IT HAS BEEN ARGUED, has the potential to refine and heighten human sensibility. Likewise, good literature can make a person more perceptive. As a practical matter, that is advantageous because the person perceives his or her surroundings more acutely. From a moral perspective, it is better because the person becomes more aware of the world at large, with an enhanced sensitivity to other people. Bad art makes people stupid by making them believe that the world is simpler than it is and by making one's evaluations of objects, events, and other people more crude.

Hence the difference between pornography and literature. In the former, "lovers" become crude, the "beloved" becomes an object, and the loving becomes coarse. In the latter (exemplified by the *Epic of Gilgamesh* or *Lady Chatterley's Lover*, say), sexuality is portrayed as a life force that makes the participant more sensitive, humane, and ultimately alive.

I N A SIMILAR VEIN, one might tell the story of Mideast pirates in either of two ways. One might depict them as mere thugs, worthy of instant annihilation, while their opponents are portrayed as heroic embodiments of moral and physical perfection. Instead, if the storyteller attempts a more nuanced presentation of both sides, the result might be Homer's *Iliad*.

And so, if Proust will not change your life, presumably he will shift some of your perspectives. The world is complicated, rich, and full — as much or more today than in Proust's time. Sex and love remain complex, as do the people who practice them. Homosexuals, Jews, and French military officers are neither all good nor all bad. Each is interesting and complicated and unique; the same is true of less "exotic" men and women.

Part of Proust's impact on one's perception involve an expanded appreciation of the role that language plays when one conceptualizes the world. If one thinks in terms of the world by way of the vocabluarly set out by "society's chatter," how much has one lost the ability to see what is really worth seeing?

Thus, at the very least, Proust should cultivate in his readers a more nuanced perception, whether it comes to living in the world or appreciating long, sophisticated sentences.

B EYOND THE CHANGES in surface perception, Proust may or may not change one's view of the fundamental nature of the world. Does some eternal Lost Time exist beyond the surface realities with which we normally engage — or the verbiage we normally use to understand it? Are other people merely reflections or echoes of that "divine" place? Is our world full of (trap) doors that can spring open and strike us with lightning blasts? Are those blasts so powerful and illuminating that one will believe that life is worth living and death is not to be feared?

Conclusion

As pointed out early on, *Against Sainte-Beuve* can be viewed as a kind of initial sketch for *RECHERCHE*. Now, having reviewed and analyzed Proust's great masterwork, let's return to *Against Sainte-Beuve* for a final comparison and assessment.

FIRST, we recall Proust's objections to the literary criticism of Charles-Augustin Sainte-Beuve.

> *Sainte-Beuve's ... method ... of not separating the man and his work ... ignores what a very slight degree of self-acquaintance teaches us: that a book is the product of a different self from the self we manifest in our habits, in our social life, in our vices.... So it is absurd to judge the poet by the man, or by the report of his friends, as Sainte-Beuve did....* (99–100, 127)

Thus, on the one hand, there is the world of habit, daily preoccupations, conventional knowledge, everyday life, vanity, passion, intellect, verbal concepts, practical goals, the spirit of imitation, and abstract intelligence; then, the other hand, there is a more fundamental world of truth and reality that lies beyond. One can live as a self in the former, or as a self in the latter, but, as Proust wrote, "there exists but little connection between our veritable self and the other one...." (VI: 436)

Here the perceptive reader may note a departure from Proust's own vision in the many allusions in this book to external factors in his life. Perhaps the only appropriate way to approach the real Proust is to focus solely on his text. We leave it to the reader to determine whether or not the external factors in Proust's life help us to understand and appreciate the essence of what his internal self was trying to say.

SECOND, we recall Proust's use of language. His style of writing, we saw, is directly related to the substance of what he wanted to say. In Proust, form substantiates content. The translation that follows tries to stay true to the winding sentences and meandering quality of Proust's original text and aesthetic aim in both *Against Sainte-Beuve* and *RECHERCHE*—albeit at the expense of clear, clean, analytic langugage.

THIRD, it is useful to review some of the key moments and concepts in Proust's writings. The Preface to *Sainte-Beuve* is useful in advancing this objective as well. Again, much of *RECHERCHE* was initially sketched out in this relatively short text. In the translation that follows, noteworthy passages are marked by **[numbers in bold type]**, referencing related passages in *RECHERCHE* and other Proust writings. Uses of the word **resurrection** (as translated) are also indicated in bold.

PREFACE, *AGAINST SAINTE-BEUVE*

Each day I attach less value to the intellect. **[1]** *Each day I realize more clearly that it is not from the outside that the writer may recover something of our impressions, that is to say, attain something of himself which is the sole matter of art. That which the intellect provides us under the name of the Past is not the Past. In reality, as happens to the souls of the departed in some popular legends, each hour of our lives, once it has died, becomes embodied in a material object and hides there.* **[2]** *There it remains captive, forever captive, unless we encounter the object. Through the object we recognize the hour, we invoke it, and it is set free. The object wherein the hour hides itself—or the sensation, because all objects relate to us through sensation—we may very well never encounter. And thus it is that there are hours of our life which will never be resuscitated. It is because this object is so small, it is lost in the world, so there is little chance that it will cross our path! There is a country house where I have spent several summers of my life. Sometimes I thought on those summers, but they were not them. There was a good chance that they would always remain dead to me. Their **resurrection** hung, like all **resurrections**, on mere chance. The other night, returning frozen by the snow, and not able to warm myself, while I had begun to read in my room under the lamp, my old cook proposed to me to make a cup of tea, which I never take.* **[3]** *As chance would have it, she brought me some slices of toast. I dipped the toast in the cup of tea, and at the moment when I put the toast in my mouth and when I had the sensation of its softness penetrated with a taste of tea against my palate, I felt a disorder, of smells of geraniums, of oranges, a sensation of extraordinary light, of happiness; I sat immobile, fearing that a lone movement would stop that which had passed in me and which I still did not comprehend, and I concentrated on the piece of dipped bread which seemed to produce all the marvels, when suddenly the shaking walls of my memory yielded, and there appeared the summers I spent in that country house which I said had flooded my consciousness, with their mornings, bringing with them a procession, an incessant load of happy hours. Then I remembered:*

all the days, when I had dressed, I descended into the room of my grandfather who just awakened and took his tea. He dipped a zwieback and gave it to me to eat. And when the summer had passed, the sensation of this zwieback softened in the tea provided a refuge where the dead hours —dead to the intellect—went to nestle, and where I would, no doubt, never have recovered them, if that winter evening, returned frozen by the snow, my cook had not proposed that potion which was linked to that resurrection by virtue of a magic pact which I did not know.

But as soon as I had tasted the zwieback, an entire garden, up til then vague and dim, presented itself with its forgotten walks, bed by bed with all those flowers in the small cup of tea, like those Japanese flowers which open themselves up only when dropped in water. [4] In the same fashion, there were days from Venice which my intellect could not retrieve, which had become dead to me; then last year, while crossing a courtyard, I was stopped short in the middle of uneven, shiny paving stones. [5] My friends worried that I had slipped, but I waved them to go on, I would catch up with them. Something more important had taken me; I didn't know what it was yet, but from the bottom of my being I sensed a shudder of a past which I did not recognize: it had been when I placed my foot on this paving stone that I experienced the disturbance. I felt a happiness which invaded me, and which would enrich me with this pure substance of ourselves which is a past impression, of pure life conserved unsullied (and which we may not know as conserved, because in this moment where we live it, it doesn't present itself in our memory, but in the middle of the sensations which suppress it) and which asked only to be set free, so that it should to add to my treasures of poetry and of life. But I did not feel that I had the power to set it free. Ach! The intellect could do nothing for me at such a moment. So I drew back a few steps to return again to the uneven shiny paving stones to try to bring me back to that same condition. [6] It was the same sensation under foot which I had felt on the smooth, slightly uneven paving stones of the Baptistry of Saint Mark. The shadow which lay that day on the canal where a gondola waited for me, all the happiness, all the wealth of those hours, poured into me as a result of this recognized feeling, and that day itself relived itself for me.

Not only can the intellect do nothing for us concerning these **resurrections;** moreover, these hours from the Past will nestle into objects where the intellect cannot seek to embody them. The objects in which you have consciously looked to establish the relations with the hours you lived, in those objects the hours will not look for refuge. Even more, if any other thing can **resurrect** those hours, these hours, when they are re-born with these objects, will be stripped of their poetry.

I remember a day of travel, from the window of a train I tried to extract impressions from the landscape that passed me. I wrote all I saw while passing a little country cemetery, I noted the rays of the sun on the trees, the flowers on the road similar to those of the *Lys dans la Vallée*. **[7]** *Since then, I often tried, thinking back to those trees streaked with light, to that little country cemetery, to evoke this day, I hear this day itself, not its cold ghost. I was never able, and I was desperate to succeed, when, the other day at breakfast, I accidently dropped my spoon onto my plate.* **[8]** *And it then produced the same sound as the hammers of the traffic controllers who tapped the wheels of the train on that day during its stops. At that same moment, the clinking noise revived that blinding and burning hour for me, and all that day in its poetry, except only that which I had acquired from deliberate observation and lost for poetic* **resurrection**, *the village cemetery, trees streaked with light and the Balzacian flowers on the road.*

Alas! Sometimes the object, we encounter it, the lost sensation makes us shudder; but the time is too remote, we cannot name the feeling, we cannot identify it, it does not revive. When I passed through a pantry the other day, a piece of green cloth filling a broken window made me stop and listen in my self. A ray of summer appeared. Why? I tried to remember. I saw wasps in a ray of sunshine, a smell of cherries on the table, I could not remember. For a moment, I was like those sleepers who wake in the night not knowing where they are, trying to orient their bodies to find awareness of the place where they have found themselves, not knowing in what bed, in what house, in what place on the earth, in what year of their life they have found themselves. I hesitated for that moment, groping around the square of that green cloth, for the place, the time where my barely wakened memory might situate itself. I hesitated at this time between all the confused sensations, known or forgotten in my life; it lasted only a moment. Soon I saw no more, my memory had gone back to sleep for ever.

How many times have my friends seen me, in the course of a walk, stop myself before a walkway which opened before us, or in front a group of trees, and ask them to let me be alone for a moment. **[9]** *It was in vain. To recover fresh help for my pursuit of the Past, I would close my eyes, think of nothing, then suddenly open my eyes, and try to see the trees as if for the first time, but I could not tell where I had seen them. I did recognize their shape, their arrangement, the line which they traced seemed modeled on some mysterious, beloved drawing which trembled in my heart. But I could not tell more, they seemed by their naive and passionate attitude to speak their regret at not being able to express themselves, of not being able to tell me the secret which they sensed well that I could not unravel. Ghosts of a dear past, so dear that my heart beat to breaking, they strained their arms helplessly to me as the shadows which Aeneas encountered in the Underworld. Was it in the walks around the village where I was a happy little boy, was it only in this imaginary country where, later on, I dreamed that Mama was so sick, near a lake in a forest where it was* *light all night, a dream country only but almost also as real as the country of my childhood, which was already more than a dream? I would not know. And I was obliged to re-join my friends who were waiting for me at the bend in the road, to turn away in anguish forever from a past which I would never see again, to deny the dead who stretched to me their powerless and tender arms and seem to say:* **Resurrect** *us. And before I got back to converse with my friends, I returned for one more moment to throw a glance of dwindling perception at the curved and retreating line of the expressive and mute trees, undulating before my eyes*

Compared to this past — the intimate essence of ourselves — the truths of the intellect seem a very trivial reality. **[10]** *So, above all, when our powers begin to decline, it is towards all these things that we carry in ourselves that we would try to recover; even if we are little understood by those intelligent people who do not know that the artist lives alone; that the absolute value of things which the artist sees are not important for him; that he carries his own scales of value in himself. It may be a horrible musical production* **[11]** *in a provincial theater, a ball that people of taste would find ridiculous, that might evoke in him these memories, or refer him to an Order of dreams and pre-occupations, much more than an admirable performance at the opera, than an ultra elegant evening in the Faubourg Saint-German. The names of stations in a railway table, places where he would like to imagine he is coming from a train car during a night in autumn, when the trees are already bare and the fresh air smells strong — a book insipid to people of taste, full of names he has not heard since childhood* **[12]** *— may hold for him much more value than the fine books of philosophy; and people of taste will say that for a man of talent he has the taste of a beast.*

It is perhaps surprising, given my small regard for the intellect, that I have given to that subject a few pages which follow just a few of those remarks which our intellect suggests to us, in contradiction to the platitudes we have hear said or which we have read. At a time when my days may be numbered (and isn't this the case for all men?) it may well be frivolous to do intellectual work. But even if the truths of the intellect are less precious than those secret feelings of which I have just spoken, they are still of interest to us. A writer is not only a poet.

Even the greatest of our century, in our imperfect world where masterpieces of art are only the ship-wreck flotsam of great intellects, they have cast a net of intellect over the jewels of feeling so that they might appear only here or there. And if one believes that on this important point one hears the best of one's times to be mistaken, then there comes a moment where one shakes off one's laziness and where one feels the need to speak. **[13]** *The method of Sainte-Beuve is perhaps not at first so important an object. But perhaps one will be led, in the course of these pages, to see that it touches on very important intellectual* *problems, perhaps most of all for an artist, this inferiority of the intellect of which I have spoken at the beginning. And it is all the same if we call upon the intellect to establish the inferiority of the intellect. Because if intellect does not merit the supreme crown, it is only the intellect which is capable of awarding it. And if it holds the second place in the hierarchy of virtues, it alone is capable of proclaiming that the instinct must occupy the first.*

REFERENCES

[1] For the truths which the intellect apprehends directly ... have something less profound, less necessary than those which life communicates to us against our will.... (VI: 273)

[2] The past is hidden somewhere outside the realm, beyond the reach of intellect, in some material object (in the sensation which that material object will give us)which we do not suspect. (I: 57–58) .

[3] This is the original version of the "madeleine" moment, where dry toast predates the madeleine.

[4] And just as the Japanese amuse themselves by filling a porcelain bowl with water and steeping in it little crumbs of paper which until then are without character or form, but, the moment they become wet, stretch themselves and bend, take on colour and distinctive shape, become flowers or houses or people, permanent and recognisable, so in that moment all the flowers in our garden and in M. Swann's park, and the water-lilies on the Vivonne and the good folk of the village and their little dwellings and the parish church and the whole of Combray and of its surroundings, taking their proper shapes and growing solid, sprang into being, town and gardens alike, from my cup of tea. (I: 62)

[5] This is the first draft of the courtyard tripping which triggers Marcel's final array of epiphanies. (VI: 255f)

[6] Note that even here the narrator attempts to recover his experience by trying to repeat its physical movements. (VI: 256)

[7] It seems that Proust will split this experience into at least the following in different volumes: while travelling by carriage, Marcel sees steeples and writes and lays an egg; while travelling by carriage he sees tress; and while travelling by train he sees trees again, and is discouraged.

[8] A servant, trying unsuccessfully not to make a noise, chanced to knock a spoon against a plate and again the same species of happiness which had come to me from the uneven paving-stones poured into me.... (VI: 257)

[9] Suddenly, in the little path, I stopped short, touched to the heart by an exquisite memory of my childhood. I had just recognised, from the fretted and glossy leaves which it thrust out towards me, a hawthorn-bush.... (II: 684–685) Also recall Hahn's observation: How many times I've observed Marcel in these mysterious moments in which he was communicating totally with nature, with art, with life, in these "deep minutes" in which his entire being was concentrated....

[10] But let a noise or a scent, once heard or once smelt, be heard or smelt again in the present and at the same time in the past, real without being actual, ideal without being abstract, and immediately the permanent and habitually concealed essence of things is liberated and our true self, which seemed — had perhaps for long years seemed — to be dead but was not altogether dead, is awakened and reanimated as it receives the celestial nourishment that is brought to it. (VI: 264–265)

[11] Recall Vinteuil's "little phrase" which becomes an "anthem" for the love beween Swann and Odette, whose source Proust disparaged. Again, in Pleasures and Days Proust celebrated the power of "bad music" to stimulate memory.

[12] The memory of what had seemed to me too deep for understanding in the subject of François le Champi when my mother long ago had read the book aloud to me, had been reawakened by the title.... (VI: 282)

[13] [I]t was time to begin if I wished to attain to what I had sometimes perceived in the course of my life, in brief lightning-flashes ... at those moments of perception which had made me think that life was worth living. How much more worth living did it appear to me now, now that I seemed to see that this life that we live in half-darkness can be illumined, this life that at every moment we distort can be restored to its true pristine shape, that a life, in short, can be realized within the confines of a book! (VI: 507)

Post-Conclusion:

PROUST FOR FUN AND FAMILY

1. Find a recipe for making madeleines, and try making madeleines in the oven or microwave. If you cannot find a madeleine tin, drop them onto the pan like cookie dough.

2. Sit around and think about other things in your life that call to mind happy times with your grandmother. Did she make something? Make it again.

3. When a holiday comes, look at the fireworks, the pumpkin, the turkey, or the holiday lights, and remember some times when they first made you happy.

4. When you watch TV commercials, identify the products they are trying to sell you that supposedly will bring you life-affirming rapture. Do they?

CREDIT WHERE CREDIT IS DUE

All passages from *Swann's Way* (Volume I) are quoted directly from the original English translation by C.K. Scott Moncrieff and Terence Kilmartin (New York: Henry Holt, 1922). Short quotations from the succeeding volumes of *RECHERCHE* (II-VI) come from the most recent revision of the full Moncrieff/Kilmartin version, by D.J. Enright (*In Search of Lost Time*. New York: Modern Library, 1992, 1993.) For longer passages in volumes II-VI, the author of this work has provided his own translations. Similarly, short excerpts from Against Sainte-Beuve come from Sylvia Townsend Warner's translation in *Proust: On Art and Literature* (New York: Carroll and Graf, 1984), while the author has provided his own translation of longer passages.

Excerpts from Proust's letters may be found in *Letters of Marcel; Marcel Proust: Selected Letters, Volumes One, Two, and Four; The Cambridge Companion to Proust*, edited by Richard Bales; *Madame Proust: A Biography*, by Evelyne Bloch-Dano; and *Marcel Proust: A Life*, by William Carter. (See "Further Reading" for full source citations.)

Excerpts from Proust's notebooks, essays, and questionnaires may be found in Proust: On Art and Literature; Proust, Selected Writings; Marcel Proust: A Life, by William Carter; The Book of Proust, by Philippe Michel-Thiriet; and Marcel Proust, by Jean-Yves Tadie. (See "Further Reading" for full source citations.)

Other quotations are from the following:

Beckett, Samuel. *Proust and Three Dialogues*. London: John Calder, 1999.

Beckett, Samuel. *The Letters of Samuel Beckett, Vol. II: 1929-1940*, Martha Dow Fehsenfeld, et al, eds. Cambridge: Cambridge University Press, 2010.

Benjamin, Walter. *Illuminations: Essays and Reflection*, ed. Hannah Arendt. New York: Schocken Books, 1969.

Boyer, George, in Marcel Proust, *A Life*, by William Carter. New Haven: Yale University Press, 2000.

Cassell's French-English English-French Dictionary. NY: John Wiley, 2002.

Deleuze, Gilles. *Proust and Signs*, trans. Richard Howard. Minneapolis: University of Minnesota Press, 2000.

Duval, Paul, in *Marcel Proust: The Critical Heritage*, ed. Leighton Hodson.

Eagleton, Terry. *Why Marx Was Right*. New Haven: Yale University Press, 2011.

Genet, Jean, in *Marcel Proust*, by Edmund White. New York: Lipper/ Viking, 1999.

Gide, Andre, in *Marcel Proust, A Life*, by William Carter, and Marcel Proust: The Critical Heritage, ed. Leighton Hodson.

Gregh, Fernand, in *Marcel Proust: The Critical Heritage*, ed. Leighton Hodson.

Grasset, Bernard, in *Marcel Proust, A Life*, by William Carter.

Guibert de Nogent and his Le Mans colleague, in *Internet Medieval Sourcebook*, Fordham University (http://legacy.fordham.edu/halsall/sbook.asp).

Hachez, Willy, in *The Book of Proust*, by Philippe Michel-Thiriet.

Hahn, Renaldo, in *Marcel Proust*, by Edmund White.

Hardy, Thomas. *The Pursuit of the Well-Beloved & The Well-Beloved*, ed., Patricia Ingham. London: Penguin Books, 1997.

Hardy, Thomas. *The Life and Work of Thomas Hardy*, ed. Michael Millgate. Athens: Universitiy of Georgia Press, 1985.

Holleran, Andrew, in *Marcel Proust*, by Edmund White.

James, Henry, in John Bayley, *New York Review of Books*, March 6, 1975.

Linden, David. *The Accidental Mind*. Cambridge, MA: Belknap Press of Harvard, 2007.

Longinus, in *Aristotle Poetics, Longinus On the Sublime, Demetrius On Style*, ed., trans., Doreen C. Innes. Cambridge, MA: Harvard University Press, 1995.

Marx, Karl, and Friedrich Engels. *Basic Writings on Politics and Philosophy*, ed. Lewis Feuer. Garden City: Anchor Books, 1959.

Nietzsche, Friedrich. *On the Genealogy of Morals and Ecce Homo*, trans. Walter Kaufmann. New York: Vintage Books, 1967.

Nietzsche, Friedrich. *The Portable Nietzsche*. ed., trans. Walter Kaufmann. New York: Viking Press, 1969.

Ortega y Gasset, in *Marcel Proust: The Critical Heritage*, Leighton Hodson, ed.

Ruskin, John, *The Genius of John Ruskin*, Selections from His Writings, ed. John Rosenberg. Charlottesville: University of Virginia Press, 1988.

Ruskin, John, *Selected Writings*, ed. Dinah Birch. London: Oxford University Press, 2004.

Ruskin, John, *Unto This Last and Other Writings*, ed. Clive Wilmer, London: Penguin Books, 1997.

Thoreau, Henry David. *Walden* and "Civil Disobedience." New York: Signet Classic, 1960.

Twain, Mark. *Autobiography of Mark Twain*, The Complete and Authoritative Edition, Volume 1. Berkeley: University of California Press, 2010.

Twain, Mark. *Autobiography of Mark Twain*, The Complete and Authoritative Edition, Volume 2. Berkeley: University of California Press, 2013.

Twain, Mark. *On the Damned Human Race*, ed. Janet Smith. New York: Hill & Wang, 1994.

Tynan, Kenneth. *The Diaries of Kenneth Tynan*, ed. John Lahr. New York: Bloomsbury, 2001.

Vandérem, Fernand, in *Marcel Proust: The Critical Heritage*, ed. Leighton Hodson, and Proust, Marcel, Selected Letters, Volume Four.

Waugh, Evelyn, in *Letters of Nancy Mitford & Evelyn Waugh*, ed. Charlotte Mosley. Boston: Houghton Mifflin, 1996.

Wilson, Edmund. *Literary Essays and Reviews of the 1920s & 30s*. New York: Library of America, 2007.

Wilson, Edmund. *Literary Essays and Reviews of the 1930s & 40s*. New York: Library of America, 2007.

Woolf, Virginia. *The Letters of Virginia Woolf*, Vol. II, 1912-1922, ed., Nigel Nicolson. New York: Harcourt Brace Jovanovich, 1976.

FURTHER READING

Aciman, Andre, ed. *The Proust Project*. New York: Farrar, Strauss & Giroux, 2004.

Albaret, Céleste. *Monsieur Proust*, trans. Barbara Bray. New York: New York Review Books, 2003.

Alexander, Patrick. *Marcel Proust's Search for Lost Time*. New York: Vintage Books, 2007.

Bachmann, Steve. *Extreme Proust*. Bloomington, IN: Unlimited Publishing, 2007.

Bales, Richard, ed., *The Cambridge Companion to Proust*. (New York: Cambridge University Press, 2001.)

Bloch-Dano, Evelyne. *Madame Proust: A Biography*. Chicago: University of Chicago Press, 2007.

Botton, Alain. *How Proust Can Change Your Life*. New York: Vintage International, 1998.

Caws, Mary Ann. *Marcel Proust*. New York: Overlook Duckworth, 2005.

Carter, William. *Marcel Proust: A Life*. New Haven: Yale University Press, 2000.

Carter, William. *Proust in Love*. New Haven: Yale University Press, 2006.

Davenport-Hines. *Proust at the Majestic*. New York: Bloomsbury, 2006.

Everdell, William.The First Moderns. Chicago: University of Chicago Press, 1998.

Hodson, Leighton, ed. *Marcel Proust: The Critical Heritage*. London: Routledge, 1989.

Kristeva, Julia. Time and Sense: *Proust and the Experience of Literature,* trans. Ross Guberman. New York: Columbia University Press, 1996.

Maurois, André. *Proust: A Biography*, trans. Gerard Hopkins. New York: Meridian Books, 1958.

Muhlstein, Anka. *Monsieur Proust's Library*. New York: Other Press, 2012.

Painter, George. *Proust: The Early Years*. Boston: Atlantic Monthly Press, 1959.

Painter, George. *Proust: The Later Years*. Boston: Atlantic Monthly Press, 1965.

Proust, Marcel. *À la recherché du temps perdu*. Paris: Quarto Gallimard, 1999.

Proust, Marcel. *The Collected Poems*, ed. Harold Augenbraum. New York: Penguin Books, 2013.

Proust, Marcel. *The Complete Short Stories* of Marcel Proust, trans. Joachim Neugroschel, New York: Cooper Square Press, 2003.

Proust, Marcel. *Contre Sante-Beuve*. Paris: Éditions Gallimard, 1954.

Proust, Marcel. *Days of Reading*, trans. John Sturrock. London:

Penguin Books, 2008.

Proust, Marcel. *In Search of Lost Time, vols. 1-6*, trans. K. Scott Moncrieff and Terence Kilmartin, revised by D.J. Enright. New York: Modern Library, 1992, 1993.

Proust, Marcel. *Jean Santeuil*, trans. Gerard Hopkins, preface Andre Maurois. New York: Simon and Schuster, 1956.

Proust, Marcel. *Le Temps retrouvé*. Paris: Éditions Gallimard, 1990.

Proust, Marcel. *The Lemoine Affair*, trans. Charlotte Mandell. Brooklyn: Melville House, 2008.

Proust, Marcel. *Letters of Marcel Proust*, trans. Mina Curtis. New York: Random House 1949.

Proust, Marcel. *On Reading Ruskin*, trans., ed., Jean Autret, William Burford, and Phillip Wolfe. New Haven: Yale University Press, 1987.

Proust, Marcel. *Pleasures and Days*, trans. Andrew Brown. London: Hesperus Classics, 2004.

Proust, Marcel. *Proust: On Art and Literature, 1896-1919*, trans. Sylvia Townsend Warner, introduction Terence Kilmartin. New York: Carroll & Graf, 1984.

Proust, Marcel. *Selected Letters, Volume One, 1880-1903*, ed. Philip Kolb, trans. Ralph Manheim. Garden City, NY: Doubleday, 1983.

Proust, Marcel. *Selected Letters, Volume Two, 1904-1909*, ed. Philip Kolb, trans. Terence Kilmartin. New York: Oxford University Press, 1989.

Proust, Marcel. *Selected Letters, Volume Four, 1918-1922*, ed. Philip Kolb, trans. Joanna Kilmartin. London: HarperCollins, 2000.

Shattuck, Roger. *Proust's Way: A Field Guide to In Search of Lost Time*. New York: W.W. Norton, 2000.

Tadie, Jean-Yves. *Marcel Proust*, trans. Euan Cameron. New York: Viking, 2000.

White, Edmund. *Marcel Proust*. New York: Lipper/Viking, 1999

ABOUT THE AUTHOR

Steve Bachmann is an author, former attorney, founder of the "New Orleans Art Review," and Proust enthusiast. Previous works include *The Harvardwood Introduction to Proust* (2013), *Extreme Proust: Philosophy of the "Madeleine Moment"* (2007), *Lawyers, Law and Social Change* (2012), and *U.S. Constitution For Beginners* (2012). At this time this book was published, Steve was alive and well and living in France.

ABOUT THE ILLUSTRATOR

Van Howell is a labor organizer, tree-hugger, and crusading publisher who has drawn cartoons for such major clients as the *Wall Street Journal, New York Times, Daily News, Newsday, AdWeek, Rat Subterranean News,* Random House, Lincoln Center, and Exxon, as well as *The Guardian* in the UK. His work has been exhibited at The Poetry Society and St. Martin-in-the-Fields in London, as well as in annual juried shows of the Society of Illustrators and the Royal Society of Portrait Painters.

THE FOR BEGINNERS® SERIES

www.forbeginnersbooks.com